Into The Blast
The True Story of D.B. Cooper
Revised Edition

Skipp Porteous and Robert Blevins

Into The Blast – The True Story of D.B. Cooper
Revised Edition

For information or permissions contact

Adventure Books of Seattle

adventurebooksofseattle@gmail.com

Main Website

www.adventurebooksofseattle.com

ISBN 13: 978-0-9823271-8-0

ISBN 10: 0-9823271-8-8

Revised Edition in Paperback

January 2011

Note from the Publisher

To protect their privacy, some of the witnesses' names have been changed, although the photographs appearing of them in this book are real and used with their permission.

The true names of these witnesses were given only to the Federal Bureau of Investigation. They were identified publicly in January 2011 by the History Channel program *Brad Meltzer's Decoded.*

The truth is rarely pure and never simple

Oscar Wilde

Obviously crime pays, or there'd be no crime

G. Gordon Liddy

Table of Contents

Acknowledgements
Our sincere thanks to the following people and organizations

The Federal Bureau of Investigation, Seattle Office
The Reno Gazette-Journal
Hannah Kanew
Geoff Gray of the New York Magazine
Lyle Christiansen
Sherry Hart
Ruth and Bobbie Shepard
Earl Cossey
Ruby Moore
Dan and Lynn Rattenbury of the Priced-Right Print and Sign Shop
U.S. Search
Pete Berg from Go-Go Luckey Productions
The History Channel program *Brad Meltzer's Decoded*
Marisa Kagan
Special Agent Larry Carr of the F.B.I. (Seattle)
Special Agent Ralph Himmelsbach of the F.B.I. (Retired)
Bill Rataczak of Northwest Airlines
The Methow Café in Methow, Washington State
Managing Editor Mark Lundahl of the Reno Gazette-Journal
'Mike and Katy Watson' of Sequim and Twisp, WA
'Dawn J.' of Fox Island, Washington State
'Helen J' of Sumner, Washington State

Cover Photos
Cover Photos: Kevin King 'Divemasterking 2000'
Courtesy of Creative Commons/Flickr.com

Image Credits
The Reno Gazette (November 1971)
Northwest Orient Airlines
Pete Berg
Hannah Kanew
Albert Weinberg/Le Lombard
Shemya Island Archives Public Domain Images
The Christiansen Family of Morris, Minnesota
Adventure Books of Seattle
Sherlock Investigations, New York City

*Due to the age and condition of some images used in this book, some are of better quality than others, but every effort was made to reproduce them as accurately as possible.

Foreword by the Authors

Skipp Porteous
Sherlock Investigations, New York

'There is something you should know, but I can't tell you…'

These were some of the last words spoken by Kenny Christiansen to his brother, Lyle, while Kenny lay dying of cancer in 1994. Lyle assured his brother that everything was all right, and that whatever confession Kenny wanted to make was unneeded.

Kenny Christiansen passed away a short time later. His family was surprised to discover that Kenny had a substantial estate that belied his relatively modest income. There was a house and an adjoining lot in Bonney Lake, Washington, owned free and clear, as well as valuable stamp and coin collections. His bank account showed a balance of nearly $200,000 in savings and an additional $21,500 in checking. It was true that late in life Kenny had made a couple of minor land deals that brought in a modest profit. However, his family wondered how Kenny managed the transition from poverty to a man of relatively good means with no visible signs on how he did it.

Kenny had worked for Northwest Airlines most of his life. Back then, they were known for strikes, low pay, and layoffs. Neighbors in Bonney Lake who knew Kenny said later that he seldom worked after the early 1970s, although he was officially with the airline for many years. He would leave for a few days serving as a purser on an overseas flight, and then have a layover at home that lasted two weeks or more.

Lyle Christiansen did not make any associations at first between the size of his brother's estate and the hijacking of Northwest Airlines Flight 305 on November 24, 1971. One reason was the lack of letters from Kenny after November 1971. Before that time, he wrote to his family in Minnesota regularly. So after he died no one in the family understood how Kenny had collected so much before his death. The only known facts were that Kenny was dead, the estate was settled, and life went on.

A few years later, the case of D.B. Cooper was again run on television, and while watching the show Lyle Christiansen realized it was possible his own brother could have been the skyjacker. The famous F.B.I. sketch, the known details about Cooper, and a number of other items were a good match for Kenny. There was also the deathbed statement.

Lyle contacted my office in New York saying he had new information about 'a famous crime' and that he wanted a personal letter delivered to Nora Ephron, the director of the film *Sleepless in Seattle*. Lyle thought Ephron would be perfect to tell the story of Kenny Christiansen, or at least help jump-start a real investigation. Lyle also contacted the F.B.I. and they interviewed him briefly. The F.B.I. basically wrote him off and logged their interview into the massive Cooper files that remain stored in Seattle.

Lyle is a retired postal worker, and like his brother, was raised on a farm in Minnesota during the Great Depression. He had no experience in dealing with the media or knowing where to begin to find out the truth about Kenny.

Even my firm, Sherlock Investigations, did not take Lyle seriously at first, but I answered his messages just in case he had something. He was reluctant to tell me exactly *what* crime he was referring to when he said 'a famous crime'.

For the next few months we went back and forth with the emails. He told me about his life, and I eventually gained his trust.

Then he told me about his brother.

Kenny's first job with Northwest Airlines was performing aircraft maintenance while assigned to the remote Aleutian island of Shemya in the early 1950s. He had been a U.S. Army paratrooper at the tail end of World War II, and often took extra jumps for the added pay. Sometimes, Lyle said, Kenny wrote home about skydiving from cargo planes 'into the blast', as he described it. Lyle added that his brother resembled the F.B.I. sketch and many of Kenny's habits matched those known about the hijacker. Both Kenny and the hijacker liked bourbon, smoked cigarettes, and their height was close to the same. I asked if Kenny was left-handed, because the black necktie that the hijacker had discarded before he jumped had a tie-tack on it that was placed on the tie by a left-handed person. Yes, Lyle said. Kenny was left-handed.

I agreed to investigate and soon found out a few things.

At the time of the hijacking, Kenneth Peter Christiansen was living in a shabby little apartment in Sumner, Washington. His pay was less than $600 a month and he had no known savings, had taken out no loans, and had no rich friends or relatives. Nevertheless, within eight months after the hijacking he purchased a house and an adjoining lot in the nearby town of Bonney Lake for $16,500 in cash. He also purchased another lot behind what is now the Safeway store in Bonney Lake, as well as paying off an old promissory note for $3,000 that he had owed for years.

At about the same time, he gave his best friend's sister a $5,000 cash loan so she could buy herself and her children a house in the same area.

These facts alone did not make Kenny the hijacker. There have been a thousand people on the Cooper suspect list over the years and some of them had unexplained purchases as well. I needed to learn more. My office launched a full-scale investigation into Kenny's life, his employment history, his known friends and associates, and his finances. In the early part of the investigation, I contributed my thoughts to an article that appeared in *New York Magazine* in 2007. This article, written by Geoffrey Gray, was the first time the public was exposed to the idea that Christiansen had become a suspect.

Two years later, we had gathered enough additional

evidence linking Kenny to the skyjacking that I put a number on it: *I was 90% certain Kenny and D.B. Cooper were one and the same.*

I began work on a book, since trying to present everything any other way would be impossible.

That was when I contacted Robert.

Robert Blevins
Adventure Books of Seattle

When we first received the book proposal from Mr. Porteous on the Cooper case, I had my doubts, although I did want to hear more. I grew up mostly in the Puget Sound area of Washington State, and I remembered watching the hijacking drama unfold on television. Memories returned of the Boeing 727 sitting on the tarmac with a man inside waiting for his money and his parachutes, while the Seattle press speculated on what he planned to do with it all. In fact, I was seventeen years old at the time of the hijacking, and I attended school in the same town where Kenny Christiansen lived in November 1971 – Sumner, Washington.

I had some initial interest, but frankly, I had heard all the stories on Cooper already. The bottom line was that no one had any solid proof. A previous book, *The Real McCoy*, had named Richard Floyd McCoy as Cooper, but the guys who wrote it forgot that the witnesses said Cooper was in his mid-to-late forties. Richard Floyd McCoy was only twenty-nine at the time of the D.B. Cooper hijacking, so I didn't give much credence to that story.

Another suspect in the case, Duane Weber, was named by his widow as possibly being the hijacker. She told the F.B.I. that her husband said 'I'm Dan Cooper' while he lay dying of kidney disease in March 1995. Jo Weber began a dialogue with Ralph Himmelsbach of the F.B.I. and later submitted some of her husband's personal articles for DNA testing. However, the evidence against Weber is inconclusive at best, and he cannot be

12

placed anywhere in Washington state or Oregon at the actual time of the crime. Weber, a con man and small-time crook, visited the Northwest occasionally, but had no parachute experience. The Bureau closed their investigation on Duane Weber in July of 1998. Later, they announced that Weber's DNA had not matched a small amount of DNA evidence the F.B.I. collected from the tie left behind by the hijacker on the plane. Jo Weber continues to insist that her late husband was Cooper, no matter what the F.B.I. says. To be fair, this supposed DNA evidence the F.B.I. offers is suspect in itself, since the tie was previously handled by dozens of people over a period of years before the technology for DNA came along.

The third main suspect in the case, and the highest-profile one, is a man named William Gossett. According to Spokane, Washington attorney Galen Cook, Gossett is the strongest suspect to date. Cook has been featured on radio and television, and has been investigating William Gossett and the hijacking for several years. He is working on a book and involved in an active investigation with the Gossett family. However, Cook once claimed that he could locate the hijack ransom in a bank safety deposit box in British Columbia, but a trip up there produced nothing. Cook's evidence linking Gossett to the hijacking is very thin. One reason is because most of it comes via Gossett's children, who possibly stand to gain if their late father is named as the hijacker.

One serious flaw in the Gossett theory is Gossett's appearance in a picture taken at his military retirement ceremony at Fort Lewis, Washington a mere eighteen months after the hijacking. It shows an overweight man who looks little like the F.B.I. sketch. This conflicts with the pictures Galen Cook has offered up previously that supposedly resemble the famous sketch, but were taken years *before* the hijacking.

In early 2010, Cook claimed to have a new witness, a woman he called 'Janet' who allegedly saw the hijacker standing on the airstairs of the hijacked jet and tossing flares into the

Columbia River while it flew over Vancouver, Washington. This claim has been roundly discounted because of the altitude of the plane (9,600 feet) and that it was dark, raining, and the plane was flying above heavy cloud cover.

In an article from May 22, 2010, Scott Schwebke of the Utah Standard-Examiner reported this story. Among other things, Cook speculates that the hijacker was probably 'testing the wind direction' with the flares before jumping. He adds that Gossett was known to be 'obsessed with road flares'.

The alleged witness 'Janet' also claimed to have written a letter to the Portland office of the F.B.I. about what she had seen on the night of the hijacking. Two weeks after that, she says, a mysterious man dressed in black visited her home and told her to 'shut the fuck up.'

Cook speculates further that the F.B.I. may have threatened 'Janet' because it would have drawn law enforcement resources from the search that was going on up near Merwin Lake at the time. In this author's opinion, the 'Janet' story should be taken with a grain of salt.

In any case, Flight 305 co-pilot Bill Rataczak insists strongly that the hijacker jumped from the plane not over the Columbia River, but further north. Cook has been a regular visitor on Coast-to-Coast AM Radio and other media in his efforts to convince the public that William Gossett was the hijacker.

I leave readers to draw their own conclusions.

Skipp Porteous sent me the article in *New York Magazine* by Geoff Gray to provide some of the basic background on Christiansen, and how he came to be a suspect. Porteous also said that his firm had discovered much more about Christiansen since that article was first published.

After reading the article, my interest was piqued. Under a strict confidentiality agreement, Sherlock Investigations allowed me to see the extensive background reports, financial records, testimony, and pictures they had collected on Christiansen. It was fairly convincing, but I thought more was needed to drop the skyjacking of Flight 305 directly into Kenny's lap. To be frank, I thought we needed witnesses in addition to the circumstantial evidence.

The next step was to do more checking locally. I suspended all other work and concentrated my efforts for the next few months on the investigation. Porteous provided me with leads and I began spending much of my time on the road. The majority of this work consisted of hunting down people who had known Christiansen and trying to get interviews. The more I discovered from the witnesses, the more new leads I obtained – and those had to be checked out as well. It was like chasing a snowball down a hill, since interviewing one person often led me to several others.

Because nearly forty years have passed since the hijacking, many of the people I interviewed were senior citizens. Some were forthright and honest in their answers to difficult questions, others I interviewed were evasive. Some of them I caught in outright lies, although I was never confrontational with them, even when I suspected they were lying.

If they lied, I would ask myself: *What would motivate them to lie? What have they to gain or lose by lying?* Sometimes this is where the truth takes shape.

Eventually, the full story of Kenny Christiansen unfolded and the evidence mounted. One of the key things both Porteous and I pursued was the concept of 'following the money' and we had much success. If Kenny Christiansen were alive today, he would have difficulty explaining to a jury where he got all the money to do the things he did in the months following the taking of Flight 305. Christiansen, I discovered, had one life before the hijacking and another one afterward.

In all of this, I never got the idea that Kenny was a truly bad person. In fact, the skyjacking was the only criminal thing he ever did in his life and he was kind to many people with much of the money.

People I interviewed often said similar things about Kenny. He was a nice guy and generous to a fault. He always seemed to have a lot of money. He liked to tell people the airline paid him very well. He made a point of saying this to everyone he knew, although it was far from the truth. He helped out runaways occasionally with a temporary place to stay and a few bucks. He sometimes treated his friends to expensive gifts brought back from trips overseas, and he usually picked up the tab in restaurants. In the years following the crime, some of his friends wondered if he *could* be the skyjacker, but dismissed it. He just wasn't the type, they thought.

While interviewing witnesses, I would usually start by showing them a large photo of Christiansen. Even though most had not seen him for fifteen years or more, they always recognized him right away. 'Oh...that's Kenny,' they would say. When I explained the investigation, they would sometimes go into denial until I shared some of the evidence from a bundle of files I carried. Many agreed that it explained a lot of things they had wondered about Kenny all along.

One woman was different, and she was a primary witness, since she was the person who received a $5,000 cash loan from Christiansen a few months after the hijacking. When I told her we believed Kenny Christiansen and D.B. Cooper were one and the same, she hardly blinked.

'So *that's* where he got all the money...' she said. 'Figures.'

This is the updated edition of the book. In the first edition, which was released in March of 2010, there were many unanswered questions regarding Kenny Christiansen. Some details were still unverified by corroborating evidence; in fact we considered the book just a primer on Christiansen.

After the book came out, it drew enough attention that many people offered up additional details about Christiansen, or about the history of Northwest Airlines in general. The investigation was ongoing, and as the months passed, we learned where we had made mistakes and how to present a better case.

When the History Channel became involved, that opened up an entirely new resource. They are very good at what they do, and they discovered things about Christiansen that even we had not known. They presented the Christiansen story on their new show *Brad Meltzer's Decoded* on January 6th, 2011. Additional witnesses were discovered, and some of them verified the testimony given by people we had already interviewed for the book.

Was Kenneth Christiansen the skyjacker 'D.B. Cooper?'

We simply present the case for it.

You'll have to decide for yourself.

Dedication

To stewardesses Florence Schaffner and Tina Mucklow, whose lives were changed forever by the hijacking of N467US.

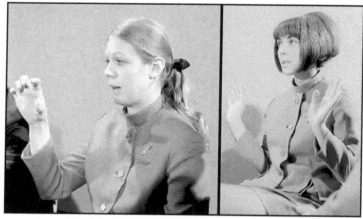

Tina Mucklow   Florence Schaffner

To these brave ladies a special wish from the authors:
We hope you are doing well…*wherever you are.*

The Hijacker

*This opening chapter depicts a possible scenario as to how the hijacking of Flight 305 was actually done, if indeed Kenny Christiansen was the skyjacker. It was written by combining the known facts of the crime with testimony from witnesses interviewed exclusively for this book. Although some items cannot be proven absolutely, it is likely close to the truth.

On the afternoon of November 24th, 1971 a man walked up to the Northwest Airlines counter at Portland International Airport and bought a one-way ticket to Seattle. It was a short puddle-jump from Portland to Seattle and the fare a mere twenty dollars. He paid in cash. He was dressed in a dark suit with a plain white shirt and a black tie, and wore a black raincoat. It was the dress of an ordinary businessman, someone you would hardly notice as they passed.

The agent behind the counter glanced at him. He took out a pen and a blank ticket. "Name, please?"

"Dan Cooper." Cooper's eyes drifted to the ticket agent's name tag. Williams, it read. *I don't recognize him,* he thought. *So far, so good.*

The agent finished filling out the ticket and handed it over. "Flight 305's running about thirty minutes late," he said. "Weather delay."

Cooper nodded. He thrust the ticket into a coat pocket and picked up his briefcase and a paper bag. He found a seat in the lounge area and waited for his flight to be called.

It was Thanksgiving Eve. He watched as people hurried through the airport, eager to make it home in time for the holidays. *No turkey dinner for me this year,* he thought.

He smoked a couple of Raleigh cigarettes while he ran through the details of the plan through his mind.

Northwest Airlines Flight 305 was coming into Portland International Airport from the east coast. The flight to Seattle was the last leg of the trip. It was a Boeing 727. He was familiar with the 727 and it had a feature that was key to his plan. He knew that it was possible to open the aft stairs while in flight. This information had come to him from a close friend who had worked with the Boeing 727 program back in the early 1960s. During testing of the jet, the airstairs had been lowered during flight, to ensure that changing the flight characteristics would not result in the aircraft inverting, rolling, or otherwise experiencing a loss of control. The test had been successful.

When his flight was finally called, Cooper took his time boarding. He wanted a look at the flight crew and the stewardesses. *If any of them recognize me, I'll have to call it off,* he thought.

He was the next-to-last person to board. He made a point to look toward the cockpit door. He saw it was open and quickly swept his eyes over the three men preparing the jet for takeoff. He did not recognize any of them. As he walked back to his seat, he tried to study the three stewardesses' faces without drawing undue attention.

Bingo, he thought, *I don't know any of them.* His heart had been pumping a mile a minute, and now it slowed a bit. He took a seat on Aisle 18 at the very rear of the jet and tried to relax. He placed the briefcase on the seat next to him and the paper bag on the floor. Although no one ever discovered what was in the paper bag, it could have been a map and compass, perhaps a pair of gloves, maybe even a flashlight. He started to reach nervously for a cigarette, and then he saw that the no-smoking sign was still lit. He put away his smokes and checked the paper bag again to make sure no one could see inside it.

Northwest frequently used the same crews on the same routes, with little crossover. His own job with the airline was mostly flying the Orient routes, so there had been little chance of running into another Northwest employee who worked stateside and knew him. Still, it could have happened. He had been lucky.

The flight was only about a third full, Cooper noted. *Good,* he thought to himself. *Fewer witnesses.*

Outwardly he tried to project an image of calm, but inside that facade he was very nervous. He lit a cigarette the moment the no-smoking sign went out. When the stewardesses came by to take the drink orders, he got his usual – bourbon and soda.

The engines whined to full revolutions as the 727 sped down the runway and fairly leaped into the rainy skies. Cooper glanced out the window. He saw drizzle and low grey clouds; a typical fall day in the Pacific Northwest. *Not the best conditions,* he thought, *but I've jumped in a lot worse than this stuff.*

He waited until they were airborne, and then took a handwritten note from his pocket. He motioned to the stewardess sitting in the jump seat directly behind him. She leaned over to see what he wanted and he handed her the note.

Florence Schaffner was used to being hit-on by men. Usually they uttered something they thought was clever, or simply handed her a business card with their phone number on it. She put the note in her pocket without a glance, intending to throw it away later.

"Miss, you'd better look at that note," the man said quietly. "I have a bomb." She noticed he was now wearing sunglasses.

Schaffner hurried off to the galley and took out the note: *I have a bomb in my briefcase,* it said. *I will use it if necessary. I want you to sit next to me. You are being hijacked.*

Trying to stay calm she showed it to her fellow stewardesses, Alice Hancock and Tina Mucklow. "We'd better give this to Scotty," Schaffner said. She and Tina Mucklow headed for the flight deck and handed it to Captain William 'Scotty' Scott. He read it and then handed it back to Schaffner.

Meanwhile, Cooper lit another cigarette and waited for Schaffner to return.

Captain Scott radioed air traffic control. 'We have a situation,' he said. Air traffic called the Seattle Police, who in turn notified the FBI. The FBI called Donald Nyrop, the CEO of Northwest Airlines. Nyrop radioed Captain Scott and told him to cooperate fully with the hijacker.

"All right," Scott told Flo Schaffner, "go back and sit with this guy like he says and try to find out if the bomb is real."

Cooper had moved to the window seat and the briefcase was now on his lap. Flo Schaffner returned and sat in the aisle seat, with the center seat empty between them. "They want to know if you really have a bomb," she said quietly. Cooper opened the briefcase for a quick moment. Schaffner saw some red sticks, a large dry-cell battery, and a bunch of wires.

"Give me back the note," Cooper said.

Schaffner handed it over.

"I want you to take some more notes for me, understand?"

"Yes." She took a pencil and some paper from her pocket.

"Take this down," Cooper said. "I want $200,000 by 5:00 P.M. in cash. Put it in a knapsack. I want two back parachutes and two front parachutes. When we land, I want a fuel truck ready to refuel. No funny stuff or I'll do the job."

Schaffner returned to the cockpit to report to Captain Scott. After some discussion between Scott and co-pilot Bill Rataczak, they decided not to tell the passengers they were being hijacked. Scott announced over the public-address system that they were having a slight mechanical difficulty and the landing in Seattle would be delayed.

Captain Scott and co-pilot Bill Rataczak put the 727 into a holding pattern over Puget Sound.

On the ground, the Seattle Police, the Washington State Patrol, Northwest Airlines, and the F.B.I. scrambled to obtain the cash and the parachutes – and to figure out a way to stop Dan Cooper.

Northwest contacted its bank, which already had cash on hand for situations like this. Ten thousand twenty-dollar bills had been run through a Recordak machine, photographing the image of each bill on microfilm. Almost all of the serial numbers began with the letter L, indicating that they were issued by the Federal Reserve Bank of San Francisco. Each bundle was supposed to contain a hundred twenties, although some had a few more or less, to make it look as if the money was hastily assembled. This pre-recording of the bills would make it possible to track the money later and perhaps trace it back to the hijacker once he tried to spend it. Some people wondered after the hijacking about paying out the money in such a small denomination, though. Passing off twenties without getting caught might be easier than getting rid of hundred-dollar bills.

Although Cooper had demanded the money be delivered in a backpack, it ended up in a canvas bank bag. Co-pilot Bill Rataczak later described it as having a leather shoulder strap and a matching leather handle, and over the years its exact nature has been a point of dispute. But it was not a backpack.

The FBI later printed the complete list of serial numbers of the 10,000 twenty-dollar bills given to Cooper and distributed them to banks, primarily in the Pacific Northwest. However, this list ran several rows of numbers per page and was thirty-four pages long. They were also non-sequential numbers. The F.B.I. has had a few different Special Agents running the Cooper case over the years. In 2008, it was Larry Carr. He admitted in an audio interview that most banks gave up trying to check their incoming twenties against the ransom list within six months or less after the hijacking. The job was just more than bank tellers could handle, due to the sheer volume of different numbers involved. The U.S. Treasury Department also assisted in keeping an eye out for any of the bills, but they were already receiving tens of thousands of bills from other sources each week for normal damaged currency replacement. They were also unable to continue this effort for very long. Although the F.B.I. once claimed that Treasury kept looking for years, a Treasury official contacted by the authors in 2010 contradicted this claim.

The police wondered about Cooper demanding *two* sets of parachutes. *Was he actually planning to bail out of the airplane?* No one had ever skydived from a commercial airliner before, and it seemed like suicide. Worse, was he planning to take a hostage with him? This certainly quashed any idea of sabotaging the parachutes. *Perhaps he had an accomplice on board,* they thought.

The parachutes proved a more difficult problem than the cash. Cooper had specified civilian parachutes, with manual ripcords. This eliminated the idea of giving him military chutes from nearby McChord Air Force Base. The FBI finally contacted Seattle Sky Sports, a skydiving school just east of the city, in Issaquah.

The school was closed for the holiday weekend, but luckily an office worker was still there. She located two emergency parachutes that one of the school's instructors had packed. But those emergency chest packs were all she had. She said she would have to call an instructor to get backpacks. Earl Cossey, one of the school's instructors, and a master parachute rigger, had some parachutes at home. Cossey quickly helped provide the two backpacks, although he did not deliver them personally. They were picked up and delivered by the police.

Back on the plane, Cooper lit another cigarette as the 727 continued circling in the holding pattern. He looked out the window. "Looks like Tacoma down there," he commented to one of the stewardesses.

The ten thousand twenty-dollar bills and the four parachutes were rushed to the Seattle-Tacoma Airport. Cooper finally allowed Flight 305 to land at 5:47 p.m. It was getting dark. Over two-and-a-half hours had elapsed since they had first taken off from Portland on what should have been a thirty-minute flight.

All thirty-six passengers and two of the stewardesses, Schaffner and Hancock, were allowed to leave the plane. Cooper specifically demanded that stewardess Tina Mucklow remain on board to pass further messages to the cockpit.

Other than suspecting something very unusual was happening, none of the passengers realized a hijacking was in progress.

Cooper then ordered the lights in the passenger cabin switched off, to prevent sharpshooters from trying to pick him off through the windows. While he was waiting for his demands to be met, Cooper asked that meals be brought on board for the crew. This was done.

Later, a Northwest employee brought the chutes and cash aboard and left them just inside the door near the front of the plane. Cooper ordered stewardess Tina Mucklow to bring everything to the rear cabin. She managed it in two trips, first bringing the parachutes, and then the money. The cash was packed in a canvas bank bag.

A fuel truck pulled up alongside the 727 and began

refueling the jet. Twenty minutes passed, and then more. The crew noticed the fuel gauges were not increasing and called down to ask why. A member of the ground staff said they had stopped refueling because of a vapor lock, or that it was so cold the fuel was beginning to freeze in the lines.

When told about this development, Cooper lost patience and made his only truly angry comment. "Let's get this show on the road!" he yelled.

Co-pilot Bill Rataczak, knowing that jet fuel freezes at a much lower temperature than the weather presented, realized the F.B.I. was trying to stall Cooper. He urged them to stop this tactic and continue the fueling of the plane.

The 'vapor lock' mysteriously disappeared and refueling resumed. Finally, the jet took off again at 7:34 PM. Not knowing the new destination of Flight 305, air traffic controllers cleared the entire area of other flights.

"Tell the pilot we're heading for Mexico City," said Cooper.

Tina Mucklow passed on the message, more frightened than she had ever been in her life. She wondered if the hijacker would try to make her jump from the aircraft as a hostage. She thought about the bomb, and the possibility that he might decide to rid himself of the witnesses by somehow setting the bomb to explode after he jumped. At some point, Mucklow finally worked up the courage to ask Cooper a question. "Why are you hijacking the plane?" she said.

"I don't have a grudge against the airline," he said. "I just have a grudge."

No one knows what Tina Mucklow read into his answer, but she may have wondered why he brought up the idea of a possible grudge against the airline. It had a bit of a defensive ring to it, almost as if he were trying to squash the idea that he DID have a grudge against Northwest Airlines.

As they gained altitude and headed back toward Portland, Cooper pointed to the aft stairs. "You're going to show me how to open them," he said.

Mucklow nodded.

While they were on the ground in Seattle, Cooper ordered the crew to take off with the stairs lowered, but they told him it was impossible.

"Okay," said Cooper. "Tell the captain to fly below ten thousand, and then depressurize the cabin."

"Anything else?" said Mucklow.

"I want the landing gear down and tell him to set the flaps at fifteen degrees."

There were some back-and-forth communications between Cooper and the crew over the next few minutes, with Tina Mucklow as the go-between. First Officer Bill Rataczak said the 727 couldn't reach Mexico City without another refueling, especially with the flaps set and the wheels down. Their maximum range under this configuration was no more than a thousand miles.

Cooper told the crew to try for Phoenix instead. They replied Reno would be better. Cooper didn't argue the point. He knew a trap by police was probably waiting for him in Reno, but he had no intention of falling into it. *I'm not staying aboard that long anyway*, he thought.

After Tina Mucklow instructed him on how to lower the stairs, Cooper startled her by pulling two or three bundles of the ransom money from the sack. He held it out to her. "Take it," he said, "it's yours." Each bundle consisted of $2,000 in twenties, although some were slightly more, and others slightly less.

She refused the money.

"All right," he said. "Go up front and stay with the others and close those curtains between first class and coach."

Mucklow glanced back for a moment before she shut the curtains and caught a glimpse of Cooper preparing for his jump. He was putting on one of the main backpack-type parachutes.

Although Mucklow had no way of knowing the significance of it, Cooper chose the older chute packed in what was known as an 'NB-6' (Navy Backpack 6) container. The parachute he rejected was a newer sport-type chute. This choice made some people wonder later whether he was ex-military, or a paratrooper. The sport chute would have given him an easier, less intense shock on opening. It has been speculated that perhaps he'd never used a newer parachute before, especially if he had only jumped in the military, and perhaps didn't understand its operation.

Captain Scott called Cooper on the intercom. "Anything else we can do for you?"

"No," Cooper said brusquely.

The crew continued flying on toward Reno at two hundred miles an hour. Somewhere behind them, chase planes were attempting to follow the aircraft, but the weather and darkness made it a futile gesture at best.

On the ground, the news services were already jumping on the story of Dan Cooper, his demands for the parachutes and money, and the takeoff from Seattle. Due to a mistake by a reporter, his name was being listed everywhere as 'D.B. Cooper', and the name stuck.

His plan was to jump somewhere north of Portland, into Clark County. It was important that he not jump too early. He did not want to parachute into Cowlitz County, the county farther north, because it was more heavily forested and he stood a greater chance of crashing into trees, or being drowned in the Merwin Lake Dam.

Cooper shoved the bundles of cash that Tina Mucklow had rejected back into the money bag. He hefted the parachute onto his back and tightened the straps securely. Then he fastened one of the emergency chutes to his chest. Although he didn't know it, the emergency chute was a training device only, and did not work.

He stuffed the sunglasses in his briefcase and then pulled the ripcord on one of the other unused parachutes to spill the contents. Pulling out the parachute material, he used a pocketknife to cut some long pieces of cord from it. It was known to be a bit tricky to use parachute cord for tying things together, but it was also very strong. He tied one piece of cord tightly around his waist, leaving about ten feet of extra slack. This was one of the last things Tina Mucklow saw him do before she went forward with the others.

Securing anything bulky to his chest besides the emergency chute might cause him to go into a tumble during a freefall. If that happened, once he pulled the ripcord on the main chute he could entangle in the lines, collapse the chute, or maybe the chute would fail to open completely. However, he knew what to do. As he had done many times before in the Army, he would make the jump with any extra cargo secured to a line tied around his waist.

No one knows what was in the paper bag Cooper carried on board the flight. It may have contained a map, a compass, and gloves perhaps. As with the briefcase containing the phony bomb, it was never found. He removed his black J.C. Penney clip-on tie with the gold and mother-of-pearl tie tack and discarded it. The tie was later found by the F.B.I. and stored away as evidence. He tied the briefcase and the money sack tightly together with more pieces of parachute cord, and then took hold of the long cord already tied around his waist. He secured it firmly to the money sack/briefcase combination.

Following Mucklow's instructions, Cooper lowered the aft stairs. They dropped a couple of feet and stopped, still held up partially by the wind rushing past beneath them. He took a firm hold on the bundle and pulled it up close to his body with his free hand. He tested the stairs gingerly with an outstretched foot, and then started down. The stairs dropped as they took his weight, and caused some oscillations that the flight crew noticed up in the cockpit.

Not as windy out here as I thought. But as soon as I jump into that blast, all hell's going to break loose.

He caught occasional glimpses of the Interstate 5 freeway through the cloud cover. The north-south ribbon of headlights and the familiar patterns of stationary lights from towns along the route gave him a rough idea of his position.

Several minutes had passed since the pilot had lowered the landing gear. Cooper knew they were either at or close to the jump point.

He fought his way to the bottom of the stairs, his heart racing. The tremendous roar of the engines was both deafening and an incentive to do what he had to do to get away from the noise. He held the bundle to his chest and jumped. The frigid air pierced his body like a thousand knives as he fell. He pulled the ripcord almost at once. The parachute opened and the harness jerked him violently. After the chute inflated, and the initial shock passed, he threw the tied bundle away from him and it dropped below him, pulling hard on his waist. The wind whipped against his face while the rain pelted him and soaked through his clothes.

The bundle hit the ground first, and then Cooper.

The landing jarred his senses and he rolled across the ground. Climbing to his feet, he quickly collapsed the chute and took stock. He was a little sore, but still in one piece. Stripping off the reserve chute from his chest, he tossed it aside. There was no one around and it was dark. A soft drizzle soaked him even more and made him shiver. He saw the bundle lying nearby, still attached to his waist by the cord. He untied it and looked around quickly, trying to figure out his location.

He was in a field. A short distance away he spotted a road and some signs, but it was impossible to read the signs in the dark. *I think I saw Woodland off to the west when I was coming down.*

He started digging. The ground was soft and gave easily. As

he worked, he noticed ruefully that the reserve chute had been a trainer. He breathed a sigh of relief that he had not needed it.

Disconnecting the harness and backpack from the parachute, he quickly buried the canopy. He stuffed the briefcase and the money into the empty backpack and then hoisted it onto his shoulder. The reserve trainer and harness he carried with him for a while, and then buried them as well, in a different spot. He hoped none of it would be found, but even if they were, the parachutes would not give any real clues to his identity. However, they *could* reveal that he had made it safely to the ground, so they had to be buried.

As he moved out of the area, it was easy to tell which way was west. Even in the starlight, the Cascade Mountains stood up starkly to the east. He headed away from them and toward the Interstate 5 freeway, which was less than twenty miles away.

Mike Watson was parked in the same place he had been since early afternoon - Paradise Point State Park. After he and Kenny had come up with the plan to hijack Flight 305, Mike had bought an Airstream trailer and a station wagon. He told his wife it was for vacations, but instead of driving the trailer and wagon back to their house in Bonney Lake, he had parked both rigs on the property they owned down in Oakville. When Katy asked him why, he gave her an offhand answer and told her the trailer would be fine at the Oakville property.

For the last few hours, Mike had been listening on his car radio for news about the hijacking. All of the stations were covering it. In fact, almost everyone in the Northwest was either glued to a television or a radio waiting for the final result of the hijacking – including his own wife back in Bonney Lake.

Katy had no clue where he was only that he was gone again without saying where he was going. Mike knew that by now she was probably going through the roof about skipping out over Thanksgiving. He'd figure out something to tell her later.

Watson sat and waited for Kenny to make it back to the freeway. It was hard to get truly lost out there, although not impossible. All of the river trails led straight back to the interstate, and there were scores of Forest Service roads and paved two-laners that did the same thing. The area was also dotted with small towns and huge clear-cuts from heavy logging, although just as much was thickly wooded. It was a risky jump, especially at night, and luck was as important as skill if you wanted to land safely. Mike knew Kenny was a pretty tough guy, but it was all about the landing – and Kenny had not jumped from a plane in twenty-five years. The plan was completely crazy. But if it worked, both of them would be rich, at least by 1971 standards.

Within forty-eight hours, FBI agents, State Police, and private citizens were combing the woods for the hijacker. Although the searchers had no way of knowing, the man known as 'D.B. Cooper' was already back at home.

It was morning when two men towing a trailer behind a big station wagon pulled into the Rainier View Apartments in Sumner, Washington. They parked in front of unit J-3, Kenny's unit. The two men went inside and locked the door.

---

*No one really knows where Cooper landed, although there are some good guesses. The Woodland area is possible, but so is Ariel, Washington, or perhaps the small village of Amboy, the place where a buried parachute was unearthed in 2008. It was named as 'extremely unlikely' by the F.B.I. as a possible Cooper chute. Although many people believe southwest Washington is nothing but heavy wilderness and mountains, for the most part it consists of wooded hills and flatlands sprinkled with small towns, paved roads, farms, and scores of U.S. Forest Service roads. Thousands of hikers, hunters, and campers visit each year, and the area is heavily logged with large clear-cuts on the ground. The many rivers in the area also have hiking trails along their banks, all leading west toward the Interstate 5 freeway. If Cooper landed safely, he would have had a very good chance of finding his way back to civilization within a few hours. Even from Ariel, it was still less than twenty miles back to the freeway.

Christiansen dumped the heavy bag of money onto the dining table and untied the parachute cord holding it closed.

"Jesus, Kenny," Mike said on seeing the bundles of cash.

"Here's your share," Kenny said. He counted out some of the bundles and laid them on the table.

Mike tucked them inside his jacket. "You never said why you put those three bundles of money into that bag and threw them into the river at the park. Why'd you do that?"

"If the cops find it, maybe they'll think I landed in the river and drowned," Kenny said. "You can't tell Katy about this, right? You can't tell anyone – *ever*." He closed the cash bag. "If we get caught they'll put us in jail for a hundred years."

"I'm sticking to the camping story," said Mike. "That's what I'm going to tell Katy when I go home. She's sure pissed off by now, though."

"I'll bet she is," said Kenny. "Are you sure you didn't say I was going with you?"

"Yeah, I'm sure. I didn't tell her anything when I left. But what about Helen? Remember, Kenny – both of us were supposed to eat Thanksgiving at Helen's. What are you going to say when you see her again?"

"Nothing," said Kenny. "I'll just say I couldn't make it. We can't be placed together on this. And don't spend any of the money for a while. The cops probably took down the numbers."

"Are you going to quit your job when we get back?"

"No, way," said Kenny. "That would create suspicion real quick. Don't worry. No one recognized me anyway."

"You just better hope no one figures it out," said Watson.

Kenny Christiansen returned to his job after that Thanksgiving week. He and Mike Watson had been scheduled to eat Thanksgiving dinner with a family in Sumner, Washington but had not attended. Mike's wife Katy had told their friend and hostess, Helen Jones, that her husband had left suddenly without saying where he was going. Katy was quite angry about it, and said so. When Helen asked her about Kenny Christiansen, Katy said that she thought Kenny had decided at the last minute to fly back to Minnesota to visit his relatives.

Not long after the hijacking, Helen began to consider the impossible. She knew Kenny Christiansen and Mike Watson very well. Could they have been involved? She was certain that the F.B.I. would question them, if for no other reason the fact that Kenny had been a U.S. Army paratrooper and that he worked for the airline.

The following Thanksgiving, a year after the hijacking, Kenny, Mike, and Katy all had dinner at her place as usual and nothing was said about Kenny and Mike's absence the previous year. She noticed that Kenny now dressed better and he mentioned at dinner that he had recently bought a house in Bonney Lake from a friend of Mike's named Joe Grimes. Helen wondered again if Kenny and Mike had been involved in the hijacking somehow. After all, she had heard that Mike was not always completely honest in his dealings. But Kenny? He was a nice guy, she thought, and he always told everyone he made good money from the airline. No, it couldn't be Kenny. Eventually she forgot about it.

A few days before Christmas in 1972, the year following the hijacking, Helen's house caught fire. While it was being rebuilt, Mike lent them the Airstream trailer to park on their property and stay in until the house was rebuilt.

Afterward, Mike sold the trailer and it ended up in Arizona. It was also the last year they all ate Thanksgiving together.

Back in Seattle, all of the airline employees at Northwest were abuzz about the incredible hijacking of Flight 305. According to some of his co-workers who were interviewed years later, Kenny always avoided talking about the hijacking and kept a low profile. He quit attending the union meetings as well.

Eight months after the crime, he bought a house in Bonney Lake for $16,500 in cash from Joe Grimes, a friend of Mike Watson's. *A few months after that, he purchased the adjoining lot behind the house for amazingly – only another ten dollars. During his off-duty days, he stopped dressing in his usual clean-cut manner and began wearing coveralls a lot and put on a *bit of weight. Most of the locals had no idea he worked for the airline and thought he was just a local farmer.*

No one from the F.B.I. ever questioned him. They had decided from the start not to investigate airline employees as possible suspects.

The F.B.I.'s assumption that the hijacking of Flight 305 was not an inside job turned out to be a good thing for Kenneth Peter Christiansen.

*The authors have speculated on a reason why Christiansen might have been able to purchase the adjoining lot for only ten dollars. They believe it was because Kenny paid with some of the hijack ransom, and he was nervous about paying Grimes publicly with more of the stolen cash. If Kenny was the hijacker, by this time he had already gone through more than five times his yearly income in less than a year. The most likely scenario is that Christiansen probably paid a great deal more for the lot than ten dollars, but the seller had to agree to either sit on the money for a while, or figure out a way to launder it safely before spending it. It's difficult to tell, but the price itself is extremely suspicious, as well as how Kenny Christiansen acquired the house in the first place. Helen Jones, one of the witnesses interviewed for the book, said in October 2010 that Grimes was a friend of Mike Watson – *the man alleged as an accomplice in the hijacking.*

This comic was linked by the F.B.I. as a possible clue to the choice of name used by the hijacker. Nothing has been proven on it one way or another. Even if the hijacker was inspired by the comic to use the name 'Dan Cooper,' unless the comic can be linked to a specific suspect, it remains only an interesting speculation.

Image credit: Albert Weinberg and Le Lombard

Kenny

Kenneth Peter Christiansen was born October 17, 1926 on a farm eight miles from Morris, Minnesota. The town of Morris is about 160 miles northwest of Minneapolis.

Lakes and working farms abounded in the Morris area. The winters were long and cold, with blizzards that occasionally reached the rooftops of the houses. Life was simple, and especially so for the Christiansens.

The Christiansen farm bordered Flax Lake, so named because flax was once raised on the lakebed when it was dry. They had no electricity, instead doing their heating and cooking with wood and coal. There was no indoor plumbing, and a two-hole outhouse stood out back of the house. Everyone had much work to do milking cows, raising horses, pigs, tending to the turkeys, and growing crops. For water they had a well and a windmill to pump the water out of the ground.

Kenny had two brothers, Lyle and Oliver, and a sister Lyla. Lyle and Lyla were twins. His father Edwin was a hard-working man with big strong arms and a penchant for inventing things.

They prepared the land for the spring planting each year using work horses and plows. A major part of the day was spent hauling water around to all of the animals in metal buckets. It was a hard life, a simple life, but in many ways a rewarding one.

When the Depression hit, so did the dust storms, some which reached the Morris area. These moved up from the Great Plains and covered everything with dirt, including the crops, making growing difficult. Occasionally, the storms got so bad they blocked out much of the sun and turned day into night.

Later, a tornado swept through the area killing several people and the Christiansen family took refuge in the cellar until it passed. When they emerged, they couldn't believe their luck. Although there was some damage to the main barn, the house was untouched – as well as their precious Model T. The outhouse, however, and most of the turkeys were gone.

Toys and games were often a matter of making up your own. Pa showed everyone how to construct helicopters using nothing but pieces of corncob and chicken feathers. You threw them into the air and watched them spin slowly to the ground.

Another pastime was walking around on homemade stilts, but on one occasion Kenny fell through the living room window and cut his hand badly. In this type of crisis, it was a long way to the doctor and mother usually took this role unless it was a real emergency.

Kenny helped out with his share of the chores, but more often worked with his mother tending the crops. His prize potatoes won him a trip to the State Fair at Crystal. Every year the entire family made the trip to the more local Stevens County Fair, and on one of these trips Kenny and Pa saw a sign in a window challenging any man to last a round with a professional boxer named 'Slapsy'.

Kenny urged his father to give it a try, so Pa did some quick training with a friend named 'Uncle Archibald,' and both Pa and Archibald took the challenge and managed to last out a round. They won $100, which was practically a fortune in those days.

World War 2 and high school came along at practically the same time for Kenny. He played the cornet and was the lead in a school play. He also excelled in track and set a school record in the half-mile run.

As graduation day approached, it seemed likely Kenny would enter the agricultural school at the University of Minnesota's Morris campus. Instead, only a few days before graduation, he joined the Army.

College would have to wait.

It was May 25, 1944.

The Army first sent Kenny Christiansen to Fort Snelling, Minnesota for a series of intelligence exams. He was transferred a short time later to Brookings, South Dakota where he studied algebra and trigonometry for eighteen more weeks. He volunteered for the Paratroops while there and was accepted. One of the motivations was money, since paratroopers got an extra $50 a month, or sometimes more, in 'jump pay'.

In December of 1944 he was sent on to Fort Leavenworth, Kansas and put through a rigorous physical training program, followed by advanced training at Fort Hood, Texas.

The Army then transferred him once again to Fort Benning, Georgia where he joined the 3rd Parachute Training Regiment.

Paratrooper training was intense and grueling. Everyone did long marches with full field packs, as well as learning the proper method of packing a parachute. Kenny made practice jumps carrying ninety-pound loads and learned how to prepare and drop additional equipment from cargo planes.

He was also taught nighttime jumps. At the end of all the training, only eighty soldiers remained in Kenny's original group of 262 men. The others had either failed the program outright or were found not suitable.

He was finally sent to the Pacific Theatre, but by the time he arrived for duty, the war had ended.

The Army still made good use of Kenny, however. He was sent to Fukuoka, Japan as part of the Occupation Forces and put in charge of the mailroom. When an airstrip was constructed nearby, he was transferred to work on the project.

Although Kenny's first love in the Army was skydiving out of airplanes, he was always a little apprehensive about it. In a letter he wrote home during his tour in Japan, he said:

'I went to church this morning. I went last Sunday, too. I had more reason to go last Sunday, as after another ten months of hibernation, I once again donned a chute and a reserve and entered a C-46. I cringed a good deal, but managed to pitch myself into the blast...'

He went on to say a few things about Army duty in Japan, including some of the benefits:

'That jump was worth $150. The nicest thing about the whole affair was that I never had time to worry about it. I was given a week's vacation beforehand, and the day I came back I only had an hour to get into my harness. The first thing I knew, I had jumped, and I was on my way back to the trucks that were to carry us back to camp. Don't get the idea I didn't get a certain stomachless (sic) feeling, because I did.

My vacation was in Numazu, a little village next to the ocean. It's south of Tokyo quite a ways. I stayed in a hotel about fifty yards from the shore. Next door was the Palace in which Emperor Hirohito's mother lives. The hotel was five stories high, and about thirty of us guys had it all to ourselves for the week.

I spent most of my time up on the roof during the day, and nights I usually lounged in a beach chair down by the water's edge. They had a group of Hawaiian guitar players down there. With the music, the breeze off the ocean, and the waves crashing the shore, I felt like a millionaire enjoying his millions...'

As was his habit, young Kenny sent frequent letters home to his family. He asked about his mother's vegetable garden, how high the corn was growing, and questions about the county fair. His mother wrote back about how Morris was growing and the first apartment building constructed in the town.

On November 14th, 1946 Kenny was discharged from the Army in the general mustering-out that was done after the war. He returned to Morris to look for work.

The crew of Northwest Airlines Flight 305 as their ordeal finally ends with a risky night landing in Reno, Nevada. Since there was no way to raise the aft stairs once they were deployed in flight, they had to land with the stairway dragging along the ground. Between the time that Cooper jumped from the aircraft and the landing in Reno, the crew worried that the hijacker may have set his bomb to detonate on board the plane after he jumped – to eliminate the witnesses. Fortunately, this was not the case.

Pictured from left to right: Captain William 'Scotty' Scott, First Officer Bill Rataczak, Stewardess Tina Mucklow, and Flight Engineer H.E. Anderson.

Harsh glare from the many lights being used by the press corps made this image difficult to reproduce.

Image credit – The Reno Gazette-Journal

Shemya Island

Back at home, Kenny used his G.I. Bill benefits to attend college at the University of Minnesota. He graduated in 1949 and took a job as a traveling salesman for the Publishers Continental Sales Corporation based out of Indiana.

However, Kenny wasn't the best salesman, and after some time traveling the Midwest hawking books and magazines, he spotted an article in the Minneapolis Star-Tribune saying that Northwest Orient airlines was hiring at their Minneapolis headquarters. He applied and got a job doing aircraft maintenance. Because he had no real experience in this work, he classified as 'unskilled labor'.

Northwest Airlines sometimes went by the name 'Northwest Orient' because they were one of the first carriers to establish new air routes between the United States and Asia. Because many commercial aircraft of the day could not carry enough fuel to fly straight across the Pacific Ocean from U.S. west coast airports, Northwest opened a refueling and maintenance station on the remote island of Shemya near the tip of the Aleutian chain in Alaska.

Flights from Seattle headed for Japan, for example, would first fly up to Shemya and refuel, and then continue on to Japan. Planes also came from Canada and Europe on their way to these same destinations. This route was shorter because the farther you get away from the Equator, the less distance it is across the Pacific Ocean. By flying north to Shemya first, it was easier to reach Japan, South Korea, the Philippines, and other Asian stops.

Shemya Island, a mere two miles wide and five miles long, was affectionately called 'The Rock' or 'Schmoo' by those who served there. The U.S. Air Force shared the island with Northwest Airlines. Because Northwest already had the personnel and the fueling facilities in place, the Air Force had a contract with the airline to help provide some services to Air Force planes landing on Shemya. Kenny worked as an assistant to the aircraft mechanics, keeping the oil cans filled, helping with refueling, or performing whatever duties were assigned to him.

There was no television or civilian radio stations within pickup range of the island. Workers spent their down time writing letters, reading, playing poker, exploring the beaches, fishing, or taking pictures. The Shemya 'smokehouse' was the workers' nickname for the only watering hole, a small bar with some pool tables. There was also the occasional movie.

Duty on Shemya was tough. Boredom, the incessant bad weather, and hard work made it a difficult job indeed. It also had a way of bonding men together and creating friendships that would continue for decades.

Today there are several websites with thousands of entries written by the many people who served there. The entries usually state the years the person was on Shemya, and what they did there. There was a certain camaraderie among the men serving on Shemya, and it remains very strong today.

It was on Shemya that Christiansen met another Northwest employee named Mike Watson, (not his real name) who would become a lifelong friend. They worked together servicing planes, unloading, and loading cargo, or whatever was required to keep the planes flying. Watson was a flight mechanic, while Kenny was a bit lower on the totem pole, but they got along very well.

Picture of Kenny Christiansen (in white t-shirt) and 'Mike Watson' (in flowered print). **Location**: Shemya Island, 1951. When a production company exec for the History Channel contacted Mike Watson, he claimed he hardly knew Christiansen and thought he was a dishwasher. They serviced planes together on Shemya for two years, and later worked for the airline in Seattle. After he was confronted with this picture and other evidence, he retracted his statement, saying Christiansen *was* his friend, and that Christiansen had attended his wedding in 1968. Watson recently appeared on the new History Channel show *Brad Meltzer's Decoded* for an interview. Watson claimed that *Into The Blast* was 'a work of fiction' and when asked his opinion about co-author Robert Blevins' assertion that he was allegedly involved in the hijacking, he replied, "He's lying!" However, when Watson was asked by the cast of the show to reveal his whereabouts over the weekend of the hijacking, he remained silent and refused to answer.

Many commercial airline pilots and Air Force personnel did layovers at Shemya. Some of the pilots made trips all over the globe, and Shemya was a key refueling stop. Occasionally the weather would bring flying to a halt for a few days, and crews were forced to stay on the island until it cleared.

Christiansen worked on Shemya far longer than most other

employees of the airline. The usual tour was a year. After nearly five long years of cold weather, fog, and hard work, he finally resigned and took a job as a radio-telephone operator in a place much warmer and far different from Shemya – Bikini Atoll in the South Pacific.

However, his short-lived job on Bikini may have contributed to his early death in 1994. Bikini was a place where the U.S. had recently tested nuclear weapons. A few months after Kenny arrived, the government decided that the levels of Strontium-90 were still too high for human habitation and the place was abandoned.

Again without a job, Christiansen moved to the Seattle area, and was re-hired by Northwest Airlines and trained to be a purser and steward for the Orient routes.

It was early 1956 and Kenny settled down in the place where he would spend the rest of his life. Now that he was a steward, he looked forward to a long career with Northwest serving passengers, working his way up the company ladder, and having the added benefit of free flights to anywhere the airline had a route.

However, things did not turn out as he expected.

Puget Sound, Washington

The first thing Kenny Christiansen discovered about being a steward on an airline like Northwest was that unlike jet maintenance, the work was not exactly steady. He would fly from Seattle to Manila perhaps, and after a short layover he would be home again about eight days later. Then he might not be called up for another flight for two weeks or longer. Sometimes his paycheck was less than three hundred dollars a month, and though he enjoyed the work it often did not pay the bills. His average income was about five hundred a month.

Making things worse, the airline suffered from labor problems and strikes. Working for Northwest at that time was a hit-or-miss arrangement at best, and Kenny was forced to seek temporary employment just to keep bread on the table.

At different times he took odd jobs to help make up the difference. He did digging for a construction company near the Space Needle while it was being built for the 1962 World's Fair, or picked apples in season, or took whatever employment he could find, including applying for a desk clerk job at a small hotel in Renton.

It was during this time that he wrote to his family:

'I've got a job during the Christmas rush at the Post Office here in Renton, but it's beginning to look like I'd better be looking for a job a little longer in duration. I was laid off again by Northwest on October 11th due to a strike by the flight engineers. Since I work on the jets, which are grounded, I am now grounded, too. So, I've been sitting, waiting for the strike to end, hoping to go back to work.

Now the peanut butter is getting low, so I've got to do something drastic, like get another job. All in all, it's beginning to look like a bleak Christmas for me. I've been seriously thinking of taking a free pass on the airline and coming home, but I never dreamed Northwest could afford to let those $8 million dollar jets sit on the ground so long.

If nothing comes along in the way of a job after the Post Office work ends after Christmas, I may just pack my bags and come see you guys for a few days...'

Northwest was still out on strike after the 1961 New Year. Kenny was thirty-five years old and a little depressed about his situation.

However, the strike finally ended and Kenny went back to work. Over the next ten years he struggled along on the meager pay from the airline, moving from place to place around Seattle. Sometimes he was able to collect unemployment payments when he qualified as 'under-employed' by the airline.

50

Kenny had pride in his job, even though it paid very little. He would often tell people that he made good money, although the friends closest to him knew better.

He managed to buy a large wooded lot in Sumner, the town just down the hill from Bonney Lake, with no money down by signing a promissory note for $3,000, but he didn't have the money to do anything with it, so it sat empty for years.

It was during this time that his friend Mike Watson met his future wife, Katy. Mike and Katy set up housekeeping together for a while and bought a rather rough house and property up in Bonney Lake, Washington. Kenny sometimes helped them fix up the property, including digging ditches for a new septic tank.

'Katy Watson' and Kenny Christiansen digging ditches in Bonney Lake, WA. Date of photograph: 1968.

Christiansen's house and the adjoining lot behind it in Bonney Lake, Washington. He bought it for $16,500 in cash a few months after the hijacking from a friend of Mike Watson's. He later bought the lot behind the house for ten dollars more.

The same house today. It was converted to a print shop by the present owners, Dan and Lynn Rattenbury. It was on the hill behind this house where Mr. Rattenbury claimed $2,000 in 20's was found shortly after Christiansen's death. This was later confirmed by a woman named Carolyn Tyner who had owned the house with her then-husband Robin Powell. They had lived with Christiansen for a while shortly before his death and he willed the house to them. They sold it shortly afterward. She did not know Rattenbury, who bought the house some years after the Powell's moved away from Washington. The house has had several owners since 1994.

Telephone Interview With
Bill Rataczak, First Officer and
Co-Pilot for Northwest Flight 305

Bill Rataczak: Hello.

Porteous: Hi, this is Skipp Porteous with Sherlock Investigations in New York.

Bill Rataczak: Yes, I know who you are.

Porteous: Do you have a few minutes to talk?

Bill Rataczak: Sure. You caught me at mealtime, but I haven't sat down to it yet. It's not a major deal.

Porteous: Oh, OK. You should be a radio personality; you have a radio voice.

Bill Rataczak: (Laughter) Thank you. I'm lucky to have any voice at all after what happened to me last summer.

Porteous: What happened?

Bill Rataczak: I was out riding my racing bicycle on a country road last year on the black top and got hit by a gravel truck. Broke my neck, broke my orbital bones around my eyes, my jaw was wired shut, broken, for eight weeks. I was in a halo for a little over four months. I'm still trying to recover from that. I have swallowing and jaw problems. I have no feeling below my waist, but I can walk and that's the fortunate thing.

I've been in therapy ever since I got out of intensive care – they threw me into therapy. I've been trying to get back into some semblance of mobility; that's the reason I haven't given you a call; my days are busy with therapy and exercises. It's not the life I would choose.

Porteous: I can understand that. You were the co-pilot on Flight 305 on the day of the Cooper hijacking?

Bill Rataczak: That's correct.

Porteous: I'm sure you have vivid memories of that day.

Bill Rataczak: I still do, some of the things have slipped a bit, but usually conversation uncovers it again.

Porteous: Do you think the man you know as D.B. Cooper could have been a Northwest employee?

Bill Rataczak: Well, I suppose it's possible, but based on recent reports about the brother of the person who was a flight attendant, I don't think so. I have not heard anything from that party that would indicate this. (This is a reference to Lyle Christiansen, the brother of Kenny Christiansen.) There are experiences that only those who were involved would have known about. I have not found anybody yet, whether it's the FBI, or the two fellows that wrote the book on McCoy—they thought this McCoy was D.B. Cooper and I can tell you he was not—I see nothing that was in evidence that would point to it. *I think McCoy was a copycat. I don't think that fellow from Northwest was, but then I don't really know.

(*Reference to Richard Floyd McCoy as a Cooper suspect in the book *The Real McCoy* – It was later determined that McCoy was not in Washington or Oregon at the time of the Cooper hijacking, but in Utah having Thanksgiving dinner with family. Months later, McCoy tried his own version of the Cooper hijacking with a different flight, but was soon caught. He was tried and sentenced for air piracy, but escaped prison. He was killed by an F.B.I. agent three months later in Virginia Beach, Virginia. McCoy walked into a house where he was hiding out. The F.B.I. was already waiting. When McCoy pulled a weapon, he was killed instantly by a shotgun blast from one of the F.B.I. agents.)

Porteous: Do you think Cooper survived the jump?

Bill Rataczak: Well, my gut feeling is—I sometimes think with my heart and sometimes with my brain—my heart says I hope he didn't—my brain says I don't think he did. The bottom line is I don't think he survived it. When one considers the terrain out there...we were flying over the Cascade Mountains. I used to run out there all the time on layovers—crew rest between flights on overnights and so forth—and I would run railroad tracks and highways and country roads and I can tell you that people have corroborated this—they have a tremendous amount of black raspberry or blackberry, I don't know, I'm not a botanist—I don't know one from the other—they have a lot of those bushes in that terrain to prevent the railroad beds from eroding and highways from doing the same thing—and I'm told that's a prevalent underbrush of the mountainous areas of the Cascades and if he were anywhere deep in the woods out there I don't know how he could possibly get through there without a pair of leather chaps or flame thrower or a machete.

I don't think he could do it. Although we hear stories from Jo Weber, you're familiar with her?

Porteous: Yes, I talked with her.

Bill Rataczak: She claims her husband took her up there by the old highway, Route 1 or 2, it goes by the coast—this road being slightly to the east of the current highway. She said that was there he walked out of the woods. Well, maybe he did. Maybe he landed close to the road and was able to get out. I don't know. I do know that our technical support people who were on the radio with us during the hijacking, especially Paul Sortum, tried to determine the exact area where Cooper might have jumped. We relied heavily on him for technical information during the flight. He was head of Technical Operations in our Flight Training Department.

Paul and many others did a lot of work trying to determine the exact area in general, and then tried to narrow down where the hijacker could have landed after he jumped from the airplane. They finally determined the likely spot. Well, our crew on board was 99% sure they were correct because we felt a tremendous amount of pressure bump in our ears when the aft stairs rebounded when they closed. It would be like rolling down and rolling back up the window with a vast crank on your car when you're speeding down the highway, which is something we've all experienced with our ears.

We also got confirmation on the Flight Engineer's panel indicating that the stairs had momentarily closed. I make the analogy that walking down those aft stairs during flight was like walking to the end of a diving board. The more you weigh, the more the board will bend, and when Cooper finally jumped from it, the stairs rebounded and sort of came back to neutral. Well, the stairs were open about thirty to thirty-six inches under the air-stream after Cooper opened the door—that's just the natural point where they will fall – the gap between the bottom of the stairs and the closure point in flight. When he walked out there his weight made the steps open further the farther he went down. Then, he was certainly able to jump from the bottom step. So we pretty much know when he jumped.

Where he jumped was up to air-traffic control to coordinate with our technical people. They plotted an area based on winds that were prevalent at that time, and then, of course, there were different approaches to his fall that could have occurred. When did he deploy the chute, for example? Did he deploy it immediately? If he did, then he would be carried farther from the jump point by the wind. Or if something went wrong and he didn't deploy at all and ended up boring a hole in the ground and is forever buried and is now nothing more than a skeleton, then he would have been closer to point of departure. So, somewhere in between is where he probably landed. With the winds it is hard to say.

But, it's strange that there's no chute that was ever found. That would be somewhat understandable given the underbrush and the terrain if it was never deployed. But, if it was deployed then it certainly is possible that he was able to gather it up and stuff it into a tree trunk or something. Lots of questions remain about the whole thing. I don't know if there will ever be answers.

Porteous: The chute was red and yellow, wasn't it?

Bill Rataczak: Well, that's a good question. I don't know if it was. That's the first I've heard of that. That's something I should take up with Ralph Himmelsbach. (The FBI Special Agent who was originally assigned to the case.) Certainly, we know there were four chutes. That gave us some worry because we thought maybe he wanted all three of us to jump with him. Then my concern was that the FBI had already tried to stop the hijacking by using delaying tactics during the refueling process on the ground prior to our re-departure from Sea-Tac airport. I thought the F.B.I. might try to put someone's laundry into one of the chute packs and one of us would get stuck with it.

Porteous: That must have worried you a bit.

Bill Rataczak: I have to say that was one of the few times that we really got a bit concerned. The other time was when we didn't meet his deadline to get everything together on the ground in Seattle—the parachutes, maps, charts that we needed, and the money of course. When that deadline came and went he became very agitated and threatened to blow up the airplane.

Another time was when the money that was to be brought in by Tina was brought in a hap sack, a bag. I'm not quite sure how to describe the bag other than it was a very coarse hap sack with a leather shoulder strap across it and a leather handle and the $200,000 was in that. He wanted a hiking-type knapsack, but knapsacks weren't as popular then as they are nowadays, where every kid in the street has one. But obviously someone in the bank had the bag. Those were times when we were afraid we might only hear one syllable of the word 'bang.' We might only hear the first letter or two of it. *(Refers to Cooper becoming so angry he might set off the bomb)*

Porteous: Did he ask for the $200,000 in $20 bills?

Bill Rataczak: I have to check my notes, I'm not certain if he did or not. Hmmm, I think he did ask for, no, I don't think he did. He just wanted $200,000 in a knapsack. I'm not certain if he did or not. I have to go through my notes again and look at that. As I understand it—this in not uncommon—right back here in the Midwest, right here in Minneapolis as a matter of fact, there was a family—Piper was the name of the family—he was a wealthy investment banker—his wife was kidnapped and they demanded money—about 30 years ago—the money was finally left under a tree somewhere in the north woods of Minneapolis. I think that was the catalyst for investment firms and banks to have the money put aside to have it ready for such contingencies. Seattle was ready for this. It was kind of strange; we thought the money would take a long time to put together. The money was one of the first things put on the plane. As I understand it, the consortium of banks in Seattle put money together for just a situation—kidnapping of one of their employees or a spouse or something like that. So the bills were all marked and ready to go. I'm not sure, but I've read that the serial numbers were logged when the demand came in. You may know more than I do about that.

Porteous: Did you actually see Cooper?

Bill Rataczak: No, I never did. He was in the back of the airplane. To my knowledge he never moved from the seat that he occupied in the very back row—until he was ready to leave the aircraft. At least two of the flight attendants saw him of course. Tina sat next to him. Florence Schaffner is the one who received the note from him after he boarded the airplane. This was the time when the jetway, as we called them, was just being put in place. *(A 'jetway' is a telescoping corridor that extends from an airport terminal to an aircraft for the boarding of passengers.)* Seattle had them. That was still an ongoing construction project at most airports.

He boarded the airplane with all the other passengers through this jetway. I remember it was raining at the time. He sat in the back of the plane, and that's where he gave Florence Schaffner the note.

Porteous: We showed Florence the picture we have of Christiansen, and she said it resembled the hijacker more than any other photo she has seen.

Bill Rataczak: Is Christiansen the Northwest employee?

Porteous: Yes, Kenneth Christiansen. Did you know him? *(Rataczak and Christiansen worked for Northwest Airlines at the same time, although they worked different routes.)*

Bill Rataczak: No, I have no recollection of it. We weren't the largest airline at the time; I probably would have known his name. We didn't have a lot of male flight attendants. I would guess that if I had flown with him I probably would have recalled his name—no, I have no recollection of that.

(Note from the authors: Northwest Airlines usually kept the same crews for the same routes, and other Northwest employees interviewed about Christiansen recalled little, if anything, about him. He was described as 'quiet and polite' by some, while others simply asked 'Who?' Christiansen mostly flew the Orient routes and only rarely the U.S. routes. He would often work eight days in a row and then be off work for up to fourteen days before being called up for another flight. In addition, NWA employees were sometimes either out on strike, or being laid off and later re-hired by the airline.)

Porteous: Do you think the FBI is handling this case properly?

Bill Rataczak: I'm not an FBI agent. It's turned into a cold case, although now there is more interest again. I had differences with the FBI. I never verbally put it into Ralph Himmelsbach's face, though. I felt the FBI was taking advantage of a captive audience in terms of the flight crew on the ground in Seattle. I'm firmly convinced that the FBI used delaying tactics when we requested refueling in the airplane. (This was later confirmed by the F.B.I.) The ground temperature was about thirty-four degrees while they were refueling the airplane. Jet fuel freezes at far less than that. We had a couple of episodes with the refueling operation that were very upsetting to us. When they sent in the first fuel truck, it had only a few gallons—I mean maybe 100 gallons or so in it, according to the ground crew. I got this from the person who was coordinating the refueling. Then the Flight Engineer turned around and said to me, "Bill, we took some fuel in, but now they've quit and we've barely got the needle to move."

My immediate thought was that they were playing games; they were trying to figure out a way to open up the back steps and rush the hijacker. The steps were in the closed position. The only access to the aircraft was through the front door Cooper boarded, in front of first class between the cockpit and the first class section. I got on the phone and told them "What's going on down there? You guys get us some fuel!"

They said to me, "Well, the truck ran out of gas, it ran out of fuel."

"Who are you trying to kid? Would you get that truck out of there and get another one in here."

"Well OK."

And off they went. Then, pretty soon the engineer said, "OK, we're getting fuel again." Then the gauge started moving. "OK, that's good." I said.

We had our own things to do on the flight deck. We had to get the maps and charts to Mexico, because that's where Cooper told us at first he wanted to go, and those charts were not on board.

We had to make sure we were going to get those from someone on the ground. Meanwhile, we were coordinating with Tina in the back, who was with Cooper. Florence was up in the cockpit with us. When Flo brought the note up right after departure out of Portland, I told her to sit down in the observer's seat behind the captain. I told Andy, the Flight Engineer, to give her a headset to listen to the radio and take notes. I had to show her where the clock was so she could put the times down—the clock was in Greenwich Time. That way if we keep her out of the loop, there was one less person as a hostage, so she was out of the loop.

We talked to Alice Hancock—she was Senior Stewardess, and she was sitting up in First Class. We told her to stay put. I made a public address and told everyone to stay in their seats, saying we had a minor mechanical problem—I didn't elaborate. "Nothing should concern you. Just relax and please stay in your seats and don't get up while the seat belt sign is on." I told her that if she saw anybody get up in First Class, to put them back in their seats – forcibly if she had to. *(All of the crew understood that the hijacker was not in First Class, but sitting in Coach at the very rear of the aircraft.)* We discussed whether we should tell the passengers that we were being hijacked—the Captain suggested we should do so.

I said, "You know Scotty, I don't think it's a good idea. I know we picked up some good old Montana mountain boys and they're pretty good sized, and they're sitting up in first class and they were on their second or third martinis. We don't need alcohol to add to the bravado of—that's nothing to take away from Montana people, they're some of the greatest people in the world,—we don't need them to look at each other and say, 'Hey, let's go back and get a hijacker.' So, everyone cooperated beautifully. We now had pretty much directed the two senior flight attendants Florence and Alice, in what their duties were. Florence was captive in the cockpit with us, and Alice was sitting in her jump seat in the first class section. Tina was back there with the hijacker—I got off on a tangent, I can't remember your original question...

Porteous: No problem. I'm glad to hear the whole story.

Bill Rataczak: The fueling problem—if the FBI was doing their job, I can't pass judgment, all I can give is anecdotal experiences that I recall from their involvement. After the first fuel truck got out of there and Andy told me that we're taking fuel I said "Good."

We began communicating with our technical people on the ground. We needed to know how that airplane was going to fly if the aft stairs were lowered in flight—is the airplane going to tip over, is it going to roll and what's going on?

Interestingly, Boeing had tested that plane before it was certified in flight with the stairs down. So, I knew exactly what it was going to do and I can confirm that it did exactly what they told us it would do. It was a very stable introduction to our clean airplane when the stairs were lowered.

Anyway, then the second fuel truck came up and Andy said, "They quit taking fuel—the fuel is not coming onto the airplane." I was getting ticked. I knew they were playing games this time—that's my perception. I got on the interphone down to them, "What's going on down there; what are you guys doing?"

"Well, you know, the fuel valve froze up."

"Pardon me, but it's thirty-four degrees Fahrenheit out there. I happen to know jet fuel has a freezing point of forty degrees below zero. You guys quit playing games down there and stop screwing around."

Finally, they brought a third fuel truck up there and started refueling. Whether it was the same truck I have no idea. We finally got the fuel and filled our tanks up to the top. We needed it; knowing that Cooper had demanded we fly with the flaps down and the gear down, and then he changed that a bit later and told us he wanted the flaps at fifteen degrees.

Obviously he had some knowledge about that airplane. In the first note he wanted the gear down, the flaps down. In the next note he wanted the flaps at fifteen. Well, that told us that he had done some homework along the way.

Let's get back to this Christiansen guy—unless he had taken a keen interest—maybe he had gotten hold of an aircraft operating manual that showed the flap settings and the maximum speed that they implied. Flight attendants don't get involved in that stuff.

Porteous: You know Kenny Christiansen was doing aircraft maintenance in the Aleutian Islands for Northwest Airlines before he became a flight attendant. He worked on those planes; he knew them intimately.

Bill Rataczak: That's very interesting. I'm open for information that Kenny Christiansen, or I guess in this case his brother, would offer that would strengthen his case for being D.B. Cooper. Ralph Himmelsbach has said that he doesn't think Cooper survived the jump. Then when you talk to people like Jo

Weber and get some of those others in here, it makes you wonder what the truth is.

Porteous: I understand that the jump has been duplicated—in a 727 and a sky jumper has repeated this successfully. I've spoken to other sky jumpers and they've said that it could be easily done.

Bill Rataczak: I don't deny that it could be done. Our speed was about 175 knots, or about 200 miles an hour. I don't doubt that he could have survived the jump. I'm more concerned about the terrain. If he landed in those mountainous woods, he might not have been able to get himself out. Again, there's always a way to do it. I would like to see the case solved, that's for sure. I called Ralph Himmelsbach one time—Jo Weber was trying to get hold of him at the same time by calling us. Ralph wasn't at home, though. Just a coincidence that our calls crossed like that. She left a message on our voicemail. I called Ralph later to see what he thought of my talking to her. Ralph and I have become good friends over the years, although we haven't talked in four or five years now. I asked him what he thought about talking to her and he said don't talk to her, she's a nut case, and she has no credible evidence to lend to this case. After about another year, I finally called her back. I figured, what harm could it do? I still would like to meet her; I would like to get to Florida. Is she still in Pace, Florida?

Porteous: Yes, she's in northern Florida, I think, but she's not in good health. The main weakness I see in her story is that she could not give any indication that Duane Weber had any parachuting experience. He showed her around where he walked out onto the road. Kenny Christiansen had parachuting experience in the Army.

Bill Rataczak: I don't have the mind of a criminal. Would someone without jumping experience still undertake a hijacking when there was such a great deal of danger in the jump? I don't know how much you've done on the psychology of this stuff—we had, just a month after our hijacking—Northwest had one where we had to send a crew down to Chicago O'Hare—I can't remember the details of it. We had a psychologist get involved in it because he had interviewed hijackers. Of course, the hijacking I was involved in was unique because it was the first one that was done for money. The others always seemed to be someone wanting a ride somewhere for some political reason, like flying to Cuba. I don't know if someone would try this without jump experience or not.

Porteous: I think some people are of the mind that it's easy to jump from a plane—the parachute will open and away you go—I think they're foolish to believe that.

Bill Rataczak: I think so, too. Another question I've been asked: 'Did Cooper have eight sticks of dynamite?' What was I going to do, go back there and challenge him? He said he did. As far as I'm concerned he did. We're not law enforcement; we're not skilled on how to apprehend someone. We have one way to get to them and that's down the aisle. Our first and foremost objective is safety. That's our primary objective of our operation, and to that end I feel very good about the job we did. We got everyone back safely, and we got the airplane back safely. So he got $200,000, big deal. As far as the FBI is concerned they had their mission. I'm sure they would have felt very badly if they had delayed our departure long enough out of Seattle to the point where he would have said to himself, 'I'm going to connect these two wires, and then we're all atomized.' They did their job, and we did ours.

Bill Rataczak retired from Northwest Airlines on June 30, 1999 at the age of sixty.

An Informal Interview with Ralph Himmelsbach, the First F.B.I. Special Agent Assigned to Lead the NORJAK Investigation

Skipp Porteous

Just before 4 o'clock on November 24, 1971, F.B.I. Special Agent Ralph Himmelsbach was driving home to supper when he got a call on his radio. He was asked to report immediately to the Portland International Airport. A Boeing 727 had been hijacked shortly after takeoff. The flight was due to arrive in Seattle in less than a half hour. When he arrived at the airport, a National Guard helicopter was already waiting for him. Their job was to follow Northwest Airlines Flight 305 to Seattle.

Word came that the hijacker had demanded four parachutes and $200,000 in cash. The helicopter departed quickly with Himmelsbach on board.

However, because of the cloud cover it was impossible to follow Flight 305. "We didn't even see the plane," Himmelsbach said later.

When I spoke to Agent Himmelsbach by phone, he was very pleasant, well spoken, and with a strong voice that sounded much younger than his eighty-four years. He was the first F.B.I. Special Agent assigned to the D.B. Cooper case. Officially, he worked on it for eight years.

Unofficially, he's still following it today.

Himmelsbach is one of the primary authorities on the case. He has an amazing grasp for details. When I called, he indicated that, sure, "I'd love to talk about D.B. Cooper." He quoted the exact time Flight 305 took off, 2:53 p.m., PST.

Twice during our conversation Himmelsbach received other calls on call waiting. He asked them to call him back.

He said he doesn't investigate the case today for two reasons. One, because he's no longer authorized to, and two, he doesn't have the resources. He said that the Bureau and other law enforcement agencies are still investigating D.B. Cooper, or as he calls it, NORJAK. (F.B.I. shorthand for Northwest hijacking) He implied that any investigation should be left to law enforcement. Himmelsbach said that occasionally the Bureau asks him questions about the case, and he just gives them the answers. He said he doesn't volunteer his personal theories.

When I asked him about a previous interview with Geoff Gray, where Gray showed him a photograph of Kenneth Christiansen, he was non-committal. He said, "I was unmoved by it because I've never seen D.B. Cooper."

But Geoff Gray, in his article in *New York Magazine* from October 2007, quoted a different reaction from Agent Himmelsbach to the Christiansen photograph.

> *'All of this makes him look like a good suspect to me. If I was still on duty and if it were up to me, I'd say, 'This guy is a must-investigate.'*

I told him about the land in Bonney Lake where the logs had been sold to a lumber company. The lumber company felled the tall trees and bulldozed the stumps into a pile, where they stayed for about a year. Kids used the stumps as play forts.

One kid found a sum of cash in the rubble. He turned it into the Treasury Department and got a check back for the bills that could still be read. Right now, we're trying to locate the young man, I told him. (See 'Interview with Helen J' for more on this)

Himmelsbach said that it would be good if the cash turned out to be twenty-dollar bills.

I agreed it would have been better if the kid had kept one of the bills and the serial number was visible. "They recorded all the serial numbers didn't they," I asked Himmelsbach.

He replied that they photographed all the bills that they gave to D.B. Cooper - $200,000 in twenties – on a Recordak machine and that the list was public information.

Himmelsbach said the FBI notified the Treasury Department and for years they checked all the $20 bills that came in against the serial numbers of the D.B. Cooper money. Almost all of them were printed in San Francisco in 1969, with a starting serial number of 'L'.

Banks, businesses, and ordinary citizens send damaged bills and decomposed money to the Treasury Department for replacement by the thousands each week. The Treasury Department verifies that they are real, and sends them back a check for the balance.

I asked him about Brian Ingram finding $5,800 of the Cooper money along the banks of the Columbia River.

Himmelsbach said, "Brian Ingram's folks brought the money to the Seattle office and handed it to me personally. It was an exciting time, and just two weeks before I retired."

Earl Cossey, the jump instructor who provided the Cooper

*This claim by Himmelsbach is somewhat in dispute. According to a Treasury representative contacted by the authors in 2010, they do not check incoming bills against possible stolen lists, due to the number of bills they receive each week for replacement. Treasury may have checked incoming twenties via a request from the F.B.I. after the hijacking, but it's unlikely it went on for years. The list was thirty-four pages long, with multiple rows per page, and had ten thousand different non-sequential numbers. Most Northwest banks gave up looking in less than six months.

parachutes, told me in a previous interview that three parachutes were left behind on the plane after Cooper jumped. Cossey claimed the F.B.I. told him this on the day after the hijacking. Max Gunther's book, *D.B. Cooper – What Really Happened*, says the same thing.

I asked Himmelsbach to clear up this point about the number of parachutes left behind by Cooper. He replied firmly that only *two* chutes were left on the plane by the hijacker. He said that Cossey sometimes forgets details and doesn't get his facts straight. He added that Cossey is a great guy, anyway.

I asked Himmelsbach if *he* ever forgot things. "Not as far as I know—as to the facts of this case," he replied adamantly.

When I asked his opinion on Max Gunther's book, Himmelsbach said he didn't like Gunther and knew all about the book. He pointed out that Gunther claimed someone named 'Clara' talked to him and provided him with all the details about Cooper. Himmelsbach says that Gunther later changed his story to match the facts.

I asked Himmelsbach how many fingerprints they found on the plane.

"There were lots and lots of fingerprints," he said. "We ended up with sixty-six good prints, but as far as I know, none of them belonged to D.B. Cooper." He also said that the FBI fingerprinted everyone who was on the plane that day, including the crew.

One of the reasons I asked the question is because my firm has a right thumbprint of Kenneth Christiansen from his Army discharge papers. We gave it to the F.B.I.

"Do you think the DNA the Bureau extracted from the necktie left behind by Cooper is viable?" I asked.

Himmelsbach responded that he wasn't sure if the DNA was still viable. "I don't know much about DNA," he said. He mentioned that DNA evidence technology wasn't introduced until many years after the hijacking.

Himmelsbach said that based on witness descriptions Cooper had dark, piercing eyes, which is how Max Gunther describes him. Richard McCoy, he said, had light blue eyes. So he couldn't be D.B. Cooper. He said the main thing the FBI goes by is the color of the eyes. *(The FBI says today that he had brown eyes.)* "Didn't Cooper have on sunglasses?" I said. Himmelsbach said he did when he first boarded the airplane, but took them off later and put them in his briefcase.

He volunteered that he doesn't remember much about the various suspects in the case.

We discussed Tina Mucklow and the fact that she doesn't want to be contacted about D.B. Cooper. Himmelsbach said that over the years many people have tried to get him to give out her address, but he said he wouldn't do it. He agreed that Tina Mucklow wished to not be contacted. He said that Mucklow already told the FBI everything she remembered during interrogation and cooperated with them in every way. He said that he respects her privacy. I said that I did too.

Himmelsbach said that he used to know where she lives, but no longer does.

(Note: Robert Blevins contacted Tina Mucklow through a family intermediary, and she agreed to let us send her copies of this book. Robert also says that contrary to some popular rumors, Mucklow did not become a recluse after the hijacking, but is living a normal life in the United States. Unfortunately, since 1985 she claims to have no memory of the hijacking.)

Himmelsbach spoke briefly about the reliability of stewardess Florence Schaffner as a witness. He said that she has identified photos of at least twelve people whom she says could be D.B. Cooper. "She's unreliable," he said. Himmelsbach claims there was nothing else in the briefcase except the bomb. The bomb consisted of red sticks, a battery, and wires. The briefcase wasn't large, he said. It was an attaché case. He said there were no gloves, goggles, or boots in it.

Although I didn't bring up the subject during the interview, my thoughts went to the large paper bag Cooper brought on board the flight. I have always suspected this is where he kept any extra items he planned on using during the jump.

Himmelsbach gave a reason he believes the Cooper bomb was a fake. He said dynamite is not red in color, but is the color of a manila envelope. He said in his career he has handled dynamite many times.

Himmelsbach considers Flight 305 co-pilot Bill Rataczak a good friend. "I never met him until the day I retired," he said. He said Rataczak flew out to Seattle for his retirement party from the Bureau.

When Rataczak retired from Northwest Airlines no one gave him a party or a gold watch. Rataczak said they removed his timecard at midnight when he reached the mandatory retirement age for the airline. Rataczak, like Himmelsbach, wants to see the case solved.

I asked him if he believed Cooper died in the jump. He said he believes Cooper plunged to his death, but added, "You can't be sure. He could have survived." He admitted that no body or parachutes were ever found.

Ralph Himmelsbach said he will be retired from the F.B.I. thirty years in 2010. He lives on an 84-acre farm in Woodburn, Oregon.

"Do you have animals?" I asked.

He said, "No. We rent out the farmland and just live in the main house on top of a hill."

Himmelsbach told me that many people don't want to seriously discuss the D.B. Cooper case. He said that too many people these days consider the Cooper case as entertainment or they just want to make money off the story. They don't really want to solve the case, he said. They just want to make money.

The 'Mike' Interview in Sequim, WA
Robert Blevins
January, 2010

In order to interview 'Mike Watson' (not his real name) the first thing was to find him. Mike and his wife 'Katy' had been best friends with Kenny Christiansen for almost forty years. However, by the time Kenny died in 1994, the Watsons were divorced and lived far from one another.

Sherlock Investigations sent me a package of address reports, names, pictures, and other information that either concerned Christiansen or some of the people who had known or worked with him during his life.

My job was to hunt these people down and try to obtain interviews from them, and the two people I wanted to speak to most were Mike and Katy Watson. The records sent by Porteous indicated that Mike was eighty-three years old and his ex-wife three years younger. I wondered if they were still alive.

According to Porteous, these two knew Kenny better than anyone else, and may have had extensive financial dealings with him. A persistent rumor prevailed about a large cash loan that supposedly went to Mike's sister shortly after the hijacking.

Mike Watson and Kenny Christiansen had met in the early

1950's while working for Northwest Airlines on the remote Aleutian island of Shemya. They became lifelong friends.

After reviewing the pictures and files, I did some checking locally on Mike and Katy's given addresses for 2010. All of them were more than a decade old, and no one I contacted knew where they were now. After two weeks of searching, I finally discovered Mike's current address out in Sequim, but I could not get a phone number. I was going to have to do a cold call and hope for the best.

Sequim, Washington is a medium-sized town on the north side of the Olympic Peninsula, and it is one of the most popular retirement spots in the state. It sits in the shade of the Olympic Mountains near a ridge that causes a strange anomaly in the weather. Most of the rain clouds that normally drench the Peninsula each year are split by this ridge and go around the town. There are signs posted by the city fathers that brag about Sequim receiving the same rainfall each year as San Diego, California. This is true, and why it is a popular place to retire. Less than twenty miles to the west, the city of Port Angeles gets four times as much rain each year.

Many people in Washington live in remote areas or at the end of dirt roads only a four-wheel drive can negotiate. I had an old 1987 Subaru wagon that I used mostly for camping in the high country. I put some new tires on it, replaced the brakes, and gave it a tune-up and an oil change. Something told me I would need it, and this turned out to be correct. That little Subie took me all over the state for the next couple of months. It was as if everyone I wanted to interview had decided to live in the most remote places possible. Maybe it was just coincidence, or perhaps many of them did not wish to be found. In any case, little Subie was ready to do the job, and as it turned out, necessary to it.

In order to devote the time to these trips and interviews, CEO Gayla Prociv made some temporary changes at Adventure Books of Seattle. I'm just the managing editor and my main responsibility is to review all manuscripts being considered for publication. Prociv closed book submissions temporarily and all books currently in editing were placed on hold. "Now you have time to pursue this thing," she said to me. "Get to work."

I drove up to Sequim on a surprisingly good day in late January and used a printout from Google Maps to find Mike Watson. Even with the map, he was tough to locate. He lived in a manufactured home sitting at the very end of a dirt road outside of town.

As I pulled up in the driveway I saw a sign: NO TRESPASSING. BEWARE OF DOG. I sat in the car for a minute and gathered up my files and notebooks, wondering whether this interview was a mistake.

I finally got up the nerve to approach the house and knocked at the door. A middle-aged woman stared out at me through the living room window, but made no move to go to the door. I held up my business card close to the glass and said I was there to speak to Mr. Watson about Kenny Christiansen.

A full five minutes later, an old gentleman finally opened the door and came out onto the porch. His face had the weather-beaten look of a man who has spent much time outdoors.

He closed the door behind him and we stood on the porch. "You can't come inside," he said. "I'm the caretaker for that woman. She's a recovering cancer patient and I'm her caretaker. What do you want?"

I showed him an eight by ten inch photo of Kenny Christiansen; a blow-up of his official passport photo from Northwest Airlines. "Do you know this man?" I asked.

"That's Kenneth Peter Christiansen. What about him?"

I was taken aback by the way he gave all three of Kenny's names out of the blue like that, but I put the thought aside. "I was just wondering what you could tell me about him," I said.

"We were friends for a long time," Mike said. "We used to work together on Shemya Island. That's up in the Aleutians.

75

Then I went to work for Boeing for a few years. After that, we both worked out of Seattle for Northwest Airlines." He added that he quit Northwest in the mid-sixties and then went to work for Foss Tugs in Seattle as an engineer.

Mike went on for about ten minutes about Kenny, or 'K.P.' as he called him, until he realized he hadn't asked *why* I was interested in Christiansen. He was reciting facts about both their lives almost as if he had been preparing for this interview for years. "Why do you want to know about him, anyway?" He finally asked.

At this point, I had no reason to believe he had been involved in the hijacking, so I didn't hold anything back from him. "There's a book coming out in a few months," I said. "We think he might be D.B. Cooper."

"The hijacker?" Watson said. "Nah, it couldn't be Kenny."

I gave him some basic background on why Christiansen was a suspect, such as Kenny's low pay, the unexplained spending, his sudden change in fortune, the fact he was a former paratrooper, and that Kenny had not been at work the week of the hijacking.

A sort of guarded expression came over Watson's face. I'm not psychic, but I can usually read people fairly well. Something was wrong. *He's worried about something*, I thought. *What is it?*

A couple of days before I made the drive to Sequim, Skipp Porteous had found out about a supposed $5,000 cash loan made to Mike Watson's sister Dawn a few months after the hijacking. The money had allegedly come from Kenny Christiansen. I asked Watson about it.

"That's right," Watson said. "Kenny was a nice guy."

"You know Kenny didn't make much at his airline job, right?" I said. "The records show he was only taking home about five hundred dollars a month."

"I thought he did okay. I thought those airline people did really well," Mike said.

A little alarm bell went off in the back of my head. *These two guys were best friends for nearly forty years and they worked at the same company for a long time. Yet he's talking like he knows nothing about Northwest Airlines.* He would have known what Northwest paid, as well as the meager amount Christiansen earned from the airline and all the strikes.

I asked for details about the loan to his sister Dawn.

"Kenny gave her $5,000 to put a down payment on a house. She had four kids; and she had just come out here from Minnesota after her divorce. She was staying with us for a while."

"Us?" I asked. "You mean you and your ex-wife, the lady who lives up in Twisp?"

"That's her. Katy."

"Your family is from Minnesota?" I asked.

"Yes. So is Katy. And Kenny. But you probably knew that already, right?"

"Yes." *Kenny, Mike, his sister Dawn, and Mike's wife Katy were all from Minnesota?* I wasn't sure if this was significant, but I made a note to remember it for later.

My questions turned to Kenny's finances around the time of the hijacking. Mike Watson didn't know it, but I already had a list of Christiansen's major known purchases that we had supported with documentation, the ones he made within a year of the hijacking. I asked him how Kenny, who made less than $600 a month and had little in the bank, could buy a house with cash in Bonney Lake for $16,500 or loan Dawn another $5,000 in cash.

Sherlock Investigations had already determined Kenny's house was purchased eight months after the hijacking, in July of 1972 from a friend of Mike's named Joe Grimes. The loan to Mike's sister Dawn had been made in either March or April of the same year. This money was not paid directly to Dawn by Kenny Christiansen. She approached her brother about it first, and then Mike allegedly came to Kenny about it, who provided the money.

"He sold the logs off some property he owned on Pipeline Road in Sumner," Watson explained. "I guess that's how he got it."

Not true, I thought. The logs were sold off years *after* Christiansen bought the house in Bonney Lake, not *before* the date of the hijacking. I did not challenge Mike on this point, because I knew that if I did he might kick me off the property and end the interview if I called him a liar. There was also the possibility that he simply forgot *when* Christiansen sold off the logs. I thought about showing him the records, but my better judgment told me to leave it alone for now.

At the time Christiansen gave Mike's sister the loan he was living in a low-end apartment in Sumner, the nearest town to Bonney Lake. It was true that at the same time he owned a small piece of land with trees, but he could barely keep up the tax payments, let alone build a house on it or develop it. He had bought it with no money down on a promissory note for $3,000. However, almost a year to the day after the hijacking, he paid it off – also in cash.

Instead of pressuring him further regarding Kenny's finances, I asked Watson to discuss his relationship with Kenny over the years.

"Well, after we worked on Shemya, I went back to Seattle and did maintenance on jets for Northwest. I didn't see Kenny for a few years. I went to work for Boeing, and then after that, the Merchant Marine. I was gone ten or eleven months out of the year," he said.

He was gone ten or eleven months out of the year? How can that be true? I thought. I had already spoken to a senior representative at Foss Tugs about the working arrangements on the tugs. (At the time of the interview, Sherlock Investigations had already provided me with Mike's work history and I had done some checking up on it locally.) The tug company representative did not know Watson personally, but he had worked at Foss for almost thirty-eight years and he was quite familiar with the shifts and hours the crews worked. The representative, who was a senior executive at the company, said that employees were gone for a week or two at a time, unless it was one of the ocean-going tugs, and then they might be out for two or three months at the most, but the workers on these ocean-going tugs then received substantial time off once they returned to Puget Sound. Watson had said he worked locally, not on the ocean-going tugs. *Why would Watson try to deceive me about something as innocuous as his working hours on a tugboat forty years ago?* It didn't make sense.

When I interviewed his ex-wife Katy up in Twisp, I found out the reason. It was a bizarre story, indeed.

I had a final question for Watson. Had he ever worked for Boeing while they were still building 727 jetliners? Yes, he said.

Watson went on for a while about his relationship with Kenny, but you'd hardly know he was talking about a friend anymore. Instead of the friendly banter and pleasant memories that had begun the conversation, he became somewhat defensive once he realized I was investigating the hijacking. It was like day and night. One minute he's best buddies with Kenny, and the next it's as if he hardly knew the man.

He said the next time he saw Christiansen was years later, after he went to work for the tug company. He said he came home from one of his supposed long absences and found Kenny sleeping in the spare bedroom of his house. I pinned him down on the date. He said it was in the spring of 1972, which put it a few months after the hijacking, but before Christiansen actually bought the house in Bonney Lake for cash. He said Kenny didn't have a place to live and had moved into his house while he was gone to sea. I knew this was not true. Christiansen was living at the Rainier View Apartments in Sumner at that time. In addition, I already knew that Watson had seen Christiansen many times before 1972. In fact, Kenny had been at his wedding in 1968 and the only time he ever stayed at Watson's house was for short periods when Kenny was helping work around the property to pick up extra money.

Watson suddenly took on a completely different tone about Christiansen that caught me completely by surprise.

"Katy and him," he said. "They were thick as thieves. They had secrets. I would come home and she was buying things like quarter horses, a set of draft horses, a piece of land near his on Pipeline Road, and other stuff. When I asked her where the money was coming from, she would say 'Don't worry about it.' That's why we finally got a divorce. All of my paychecks were going straight to her when I was in the Merchant Marine…'

I could hardly keep up with him as he went on about these things, little of which I actually believed. After a while, I detected a pattern in what he was saying.

He was trying to deflect any possible suspicion about Christiansen's activities or any questions about money away from himself and onto his ex-wife.

He asked if I was planning to interview Katy up in Twisp. I said yes.

He volunteered to accompany me up to Twisp, which is a good 350 miles from Sequim. I knew this wasn't a good idea. According to court records, their divorce took years to settle and was extremely bitter. I already had Katy's address in Twisp, although finding its exact location on maps was proving to be tricky.

However, when I declined his offer of company and asked him instead how to find Katy's little ranch in Twisp, he said he didn't know where she lived; only the Post Office box she used in town. I was aware that Watson knew *exactly* where she lived, since according to records from the Washington State Department of Ecology; he had once applied for a permit to dig a well on the property and had done some of the work himself. He had also lived there with Katy before the divorce. He promised to send me some pictures of him and Kenny later. I asked for his phone number, but he refused to give it to me and closed the door rather abruptly. I never received the pictures, but then I never really expected to get them. I began to suspect he was either involved in the hijacking somehow, or else he knew more than he was saying.

On the long drive back to my office in Auburn, I called Skipp Porteous and told him we might be onto something, but that more investigation was necessary. He replied that he had more people he wanted me to interview, and that he would be sending their names to me.

The next day I met with Gayla Prociv. She examined my notes and we discussed the situation. "All right," she said, "I'm putting a complete freeze on any outgoing information regarding this book. Nothing goes out to the press or the public, and I mean *nothing*." She decided that only I, Greg Page from Microsoft, and Geoff Nelder of Great Britain would be in the loop. "If word gets out that we might have viable witnesses in the Cooper case," she said, "reporters might start hounding them before we can get their statements. So nothing goes out." She also made the decision that we would change the names of some of the witnesses for the book and only give their true names to the Seattle office of the F.B.I.

Prociv was also worried that if the Seattle F.B.I. found out what we were doing, that they might come to our office with a warrant and confiscate all of the files, records, pictures, and other documents we had on Kenny Christiansen, maybe even our computers. This fear later turned out to be groundless. The F.B.I. had put the case on the back burner a long time ago.

'Katy' in January 2010.

The First Interview with 'Katy Watson'

Twisp, Washington is a remote little town in the north central part of the state. As I checked my maps in preparation to make the 250-mile drive from my office in Auburn, I tried to find some local background on 'Katy' before committing to such a long drive. If I could obtain her number, perhaps asking for the interview over the phone instead of just showing up in her driveway might have better results.

I called a reporter at the Methow Valley News in Twisp and he perked up right away when I asked him what he knew about 'Katy'. I gave him her real name, of course.

"Eccentric, but harmless," was how he described the eighty-year old woman. She lived alone, he said, on a small ranch a few miles outside of town.

I was planning to drive up that coming Saturday, so during the week I exchanged phone calls and emails with this reporter in an effort to gain his trust and convince him to accompany me to Katy's house as a go-between. However, when I finally revealed to him why I wanted to interview Katy, he backed away from the whole thing. He didn't want to get involved, he said.

When I asked him why, he said it was a small town and everybody knew everybody. He didn't want to be the one who possibly implicated Katy, a long-term resident, of being involved in the hijacking. I assured him that my interview would be friendly and completely non-threatening, but he would have nothing to do with it. I was on my own and would have to do another cold-call interview.

I discussed his refusal with Gayla Prociv. She said he didn't sound like much of a newspaper reporter, since he had no interest in a possible local connection to one of the biggest unsolved crimes in history. I had to agree.

The reporter also warned me that Katy's house had been broken into a couple of times, and that she might answer the door holding a shotgun.

In order to reach Twisp in winter, you have to cross both Snoqualmie Pass and Blewett Pass in the snow. I packed up my old Subaru wagon with tire chains, a sleeping bag, tools, and plenty of emergency gear, along with my camera and notebooks. I knew it was going to be a tough drive in the winter weather.

Commitments during the workweek narrowed my window for the trip from Friday night to Sunday night. I had less than sixty hours to make a five-hundred-mile round trip, cross a total of four mountain passes, and get the interview and some pictures. A tall order indeed, but I changed my clothes from casual to heavy winter wear and prepared for the drive.

The old (but reliable) 1987 Subaru 4WD I used to hunt down the witnesses.
Picture taken during the fifth and final interview of 'Katy' in October 2010.

I left Auburn on Friday afternoon after a full day's work, but it was already getting dark by the time I reached the summit of Snoqualmie Pass. The long week had drained me and I was falling asleep at the wheel as I made it down to Cle Elum, the first real town on the other side of the Cascades.

I pulled into a Burger King and ordered some food and a cup of coffee. As I sat at the table, I was near exhaustion. I knew I would never make it over the next mountain pass without running off the road or plunging into a snowy ravine. I decided to drive on to Blewett Pass anyway, and then find one of the many Forest Service roads near the summit and pull over for some sleep.

After driving for another hour or so, I finally reached the summit and spotted the road I wanted. I put the Subie into four-wheel-drive and forced it about a quarter of a mile off the main highway through six inches of snow. I found a ranger station that was closed for the winter and pulled in under a big cedar.

Climbing into the back of the wagon, I cracked the windows for air and found my sleeping bag. Five minutes later I was asleep.

The next morning I woke up so sore and chilled from sleeping in the back of the wagon that I swore the next time I would plan on a motel room instead. I had forgotten this wasn't just another camping trip. Before I got involved in the Cooper case, I spent a lot of my free time in that old Subaru cruising into the high country all over the state. That had come to an end lately, since I was now running around more than a chicken at a fox convention.

I snapped a few pictures for the files and plowed through the snow back down to the main road. It was Saturday morning and the highway was buzzing with pickup trucks pulling trailers. On the trailers sat snowmobiles.

Although the road was steep and slippery, many of these drivers were trying to get to the snowmobile trail jump-off points along the summit of the pass and they drove like madmen through the slush. I had to pull off the road a few times and allow them to blast my car with wet snow as they zoomed past.

An hour later I was back on the flatlands and the snow turned to light rain. As I drove the two-lane highway north to Ellensburg, the hub of Washington's apple industry, I saw dozens of orchards. They were fields of stark black fingers pointing to a cold, grey sky. On the other side of Ellensburg, a much newer Subaru Outback wagon raced around me at a high rate of speed, nearly snapping off my driver's side mirror. Five minutes later I passed this same Outback as it sat on the side of the road.

The car was pulled over to the shoulder and the front end was completely wrecked. The radiator steamed as the anti-freeze poured out onto the road. I saw the driver standing near the front of his car and looking at the damage.

A dead deer on the centerline told the story. In this area of Washington there are the same signs everywhere: *Warning! Wildlife Crossing*. He hadn't paid attention.

The drive to Twisp was long and lonely. Two hours later I pulled into town. I was tired and hungry so I parked in front of the first restaurant I found and collapsed into a chair at a corner table.

After ordering some breakfast, I headed to the rear of the old restaurant to use the bathroom. I saw buckets in the hallway to catch the leaks from the roof, and realized the whole place was in pretty bad shape. The ceilings sagged and everything was old. I knew that within a few years the place would no longer exist. The cold and wet of the North Cascades had finally beaten it down to a semblance of its former glory, and now it was just a tired, old restaurant.

The food was good though and the waitress a charmer. I tipped her five dollars.

Although I had Katy Watson's address, I was still apprehensive about approaching her house. I checked my notebooks and camera, and then marked a spot on the map where I guessed her house was located. It was almost noon and time to give it a try.

I drove out of town a few miles and found the road named on the map. However, the only hints of any address were on mailboxes, and some of them were in poor condition or the writing barely visible. The postman, of course, probably knew the route by heart.

After a few back and forth trips down this old country road, I finally spotted Katy Watson's house. It was a brick ranch affair set off some distance from the road. The long driveway was buried in wet muddy snow. I put the Subie wagon into four-wheel low and wallowed through the mud-snow toward the house. I pulled up next to an old truck and stopped.

A small German shepherd watched me from behind the confines of a fenced-off dog run attached to the rear of the house. It didn't bark; it simply stared at me and wagged its tail. I gathered up my equipment and walked to the back door. I waved at the dog. At the other end of the property was the biggest horse I'd ever seen, a gigantic draft animal the size of a Budweiser Clydesdale. You would need a ladder to mount it. The horse pawed against the fence and waved its head at me.

There was a ship's bell attached to the back door with a 'Ring Me' sign. I rang it gently as I could and hoped for the best.

A pleasant-looking lady with white hair and a friendly face opened the door.

"Hi, my name's Robert Blevins," I said. "I'm with Adventure Books of Seattle."

"Are you a salesman?" she said. "I don't really need any books."

"No, ma'am." I held up my eight-by-ten photo of Kenny Christiansen, the one we blew up from his passport picture. "Do you know this man?"

"Oh, sure. That's Kenny. But he's been dead for a long time now."

"Yes, ma'am. I know. We're doing a book about him and I heard you knew him pretty well," I said. "I just wanted to ask you some questions about his life."

She opened the screen door and I went inside. She invited me to sit down at the dining room table and poured us some tea.

"Why are you doing a book about Kenny?" She asked.

On some of the interviews I did, such as the one later with 'Dawn J,' I tried to avoid saying we were investigating Kenny as being the hijacker. I saw right away this wasn't going to work with Katy Watson, who was a get-to-the-point type of woman. Taking out my file package, I showed her a few pictures and documents. Some were related to the D.B. Cooper case, others to Kenny. She got the idea at once.

"We believe Kenny and the skyjacker known as 'D.B. Cooper' might be one and the same," I said.

From my previous interviews with people who had known the Watsons, I understood Katy and Mike had been extremely good friends with Christiansen, so I didn't know what reaction to expect by telling her that a man she had been friends with for decades might be a criminal. *Maybe she will just throw me out of the house,* I thought.

"Kenny?" She said, pouring herself some more tea. "You really think he was D.B. Cooper?"

I took a casual glance around the house. Although the dishes were washed and the place was uncluttered, the dust on the floors and furniture was thick enough to write your name in it. The house had not been cleaned properly in a very long time, although the place was livable enough. There were pictures of Katy driving some big draft horses and a wagon, picture frames made from old horseshoes, and strangely, padlocks and hasps fastened on some of the interior doors of the house. I asked her the purpose of the locks.

"My ex broke in here once," she said. "He took important papers. Now I don't have clear title to this place anymore, and he sold off some of the land to the D.N.R. without telling me."

The Department of Natural Resources was the Washington State version of the Forest Service. They controlled much of the state-owned lands. I asked when the break-in happened. She said it was in 1994, right after Kenny Christiansen died of cancer.

Katy and I talked about how she met Christiansen, and the relationship between her, the ex-husband, and Kenny. She wandered a lot and was a little confused about dates. When I tried to pin her down about events around the date of the hijacking, she would change the subject to something that happened years before the hijacking or closer to the present.

I couldn't tell if she was doing this on purpose or because she couldn't remember. It was frustrating to interview her, although I tried to be patient. She went on for a long time about Mike's theft of the documents ('he's nothing but a crook') and told me she had written to a female F.B.I. agent in Spokane about it. From what I could gather, the agent had spoken to Katy once long ago, but since that time had ignored her letters.

Katy and I spoke for another hour. It was the most difficult interview I've ever done. In direct opposition to what her ex-husband had said, Katy pointed to him as a possible accomplice in the hijacking. "He was a crook," she said about Mike, also naming a couple of his friends she claimed were involved in dubious activities.

Trying to keep her focused on the time just before the hijacking was almost impossible. When I would ask a direct question about events in that time frame, she often ignored the question or went off on another tangent about the female F.B.I. agent in Spokane. I wondered if she were what the psych experts called a 'borderline personality' or perhaps she was having difficulty concentrating because she lived alone and was getting along in years. I couldn't be sure.

A more likely possibility was the issue of trust. Maybe she wasn't ready to reveal everything to a stranger who had just showed up at her door without an invitation, asking questions about things that happened forty years ago. I knew I was going to have to do another interview with her, and I would have to come better prepared next time.

As I plodded through the mud-snow back out to my car, she came outside and surprised me with a strange question. "You're not going to make Kenny look bad, are you?" She asked. "No matter what he may have done, he was a nice guy."

"No ma'am," I said. That was the truth. I generally considered Christiansen, if he were the hijacker, as only a frustrated man who finally stuck it to his employers.

The drive home from Twisp was a little easier. The snow had stopped and the sky was clear. I made it back to Auburn as it was getting dark and went upstairs to my office. I was dead tired and ready to sleep for the next twenty-four hours, but I had one more thing to do.

I wrote a letter to Katy Watson asking for a second interview on the following Saturday and had it sent next-day delivery. An answer came on the following Thursday.

She agreed to see me again.

The Interview with 'Dawn J'
Robert Blevins

Mike Watson's sister, a very sweet lady indeed, lives on Fox Island near the city of Tacoma. Like most of the people I interviewed, it was to be a cold-call since everyone on the interview list either had no phone or their numbers were unlisted. Since I was due to drive up to Twisp that coming weekend to do a second interview with Katy Watson, I decided to try and interview Dawn during the week. Perhaps she could provide some information that would help me in my next interview with Katy, since she was Katy's former sister-in-law.

A strapping young gentleman who resembled a bodyguard answered the door when I knocked. He could have been a linebacker for the Seattle Seahawks football team. His name was Jonathan and he was Dawn's grandson. He was helping take care of her, he said.

I told him I was doing research on a man Dawn once knew and gave him the Christiansen passport photograph to show her.

He disappeared inside the house for a moment. He returned shortly and held open the door. "Come on in," he said. "She says she'll talk to you."

Unlike Katy Watson, Dawn had no problem answering questions. From the beginning, there was a twinkle in her eye that told me she knew a lot about Christiansen. At first, I avoided mentioning the possible connection between Christiansen and D.B. Cooper and I just told her I was doing a biography of Christiansen and wanted to clear up some points on his life. After my interview with her brother, I'd decided this was a better approach, since bringing up the Cooper case sometimes put people on the defensive. I asked whether she had received a $5,000 cash loan from Kenny in early 1972.

"Yes. He gave it to Mike and then Mike gave it to me," she said. "I used it to put a down payment on a house in Sumner. Kenny said I could have four years to pay it back, but I paid it back in two."

"How do you think Kenny got the money?" I asked.

"His job I suppose," she said. "He told everyone he made good money at Northwest."

"At the time he gave the loan," I said, "he was taking home less than six hundred a month."

She was mildly surprised at this. "Well, I don't know. He just told people he made a lot of money with the airline." She pointed to a very nice clock on the wall. "He gave me that as a gift after one of his trips to Japan."

It was an expensive-looking, handmade cuckoo clock. I asked if she had received the clock after 1971. She said yes.

I took out a photo that I had downloaded from the Seattle F.B.I.'s website entry on the D.B. Cooper case. It was a large picture of the black J.C. Penney tie with the mother-of-pearl tie clasp that the hijacker had left behind before he jumped. It was not labeled or anything, just a simple picture. I pushed the photo across the table. "Does this mean anything to you?" I said.

"Well, I don't know about the tie," she replied, "but I saw

Kenny wearing that tie tack a couple of times."

"Are you sure?" I said.

"Oh, yes. He had one just like it."

I could hardly believe my ears. No one had ever linked the tie or the clip to a specific person before, and Dawn had just dropped an ID on it as casually as anything. And she had done it before she understood the significance of it. *I hadn't told her anything yet about Kenny being a suspect in the hijacking.*

It was time to break the ice. I told her straight out that Kenny Christiansen was being investigated for possibly being involved in the Cooper hijacking. I discussed some of the basic evidence that had come to light, such as Kenny being in the paratroops, and the unexplained spending. Instead of a shocked reaction, she smiled. "Could be true," she said. "It would explain a lot of things people wondered about Kenny."

I asked her if she had ever suspected that Kenny Christiansen could be D.B. Cooper.

"Yes. I wasn't the only one who wondered about it either," she said.

"I don't understand," I said. "You mean other people suspected he was the hijacker, too?"

"Friends. Some of us were friends back then up in Bonney Lake. We did things together. Now everybody's gone, or moved," she explained. "Kenny never talked about the hijacking. I always thought that was strange because everyone talked about it for months, and he worked for the airline, so you would think he might have an opinion. But he never said a word about it."

"Some of the people he worked with at Northwest said the same thing," I said. "Why didn't any of you ask him if he was the guy?"

"Oh, we couldn't do that. It would have been bad manners," she said. "He worked for the airline and he was a nice man. No one was going to ask something like that to his face. Besides, he didn't look like a criminal. You said he was a paratrooper in the Army?"

"Yes, ma'am."

"Funny he never said anything about it. How sure are you that Kenny was D.B. Cooper?" She said.

"Maybe sixty, maybe seventy percent," I said. "The investigation is still ongoing."

"So *that's* where he got all that money," she said. "Figures."

We talked about Christiansen casually for another half-hour and I showed her some of the files and pictures from Sherlock Investigations. Although I was convinced she really did not know for sure if Kenny was the hijacker, she did give me a few key pieces of information.

She said yes when I asked her if Kenny was left-handed. (*The tie was likely worn by somebody who was left-handed, because the tie tack on it was slipped on from the left side. A rightie would have to turn their hand around to put it on that way.*) I asked her if Kenny had ever worn a toupee. She said yes, but added that he never wore it on the job, only socially sometimes and not very often. I pinned her down on the last time she had actually seen him wear it. No, she said, she had not seen him wear it after 1971. He had taken to wearing baseball hats instead.

I told her that I had already interviewed her former sister-in-law up in Twisp, and that I was planning another interview with Katy that coming weekend.

"Oh, she probably knows *something*," Dawn said. "She and Kenny were pretty close. I know he made a trip up there to see her in 1994, just before he died."

I asked what she knew about her brother Mike and his relationship with Kenny. She said Mike and Kenny had been friends for many years, but there was a falling-out between them in the 1970's. When I asked her if this falling-out was before or after the hijacking, she said it was a year or so afterward, although Kenny continued seeing Katy Watson when Mike was off on the tugboats for a few days. They would play cards, or just hang out with Katy's other friends, and sometimes she was included. Occasionally they had parties or went to the beach.

Dawn also said that Kenny worked much less after the hijacking and was often dressed in farm coveralls when he wasn't working.

I avoided telling her that Skipp Porteous and I now considered her brother Mike a possible accomplice. Unless we could prove it somehow, there didn't seem to be any point.

As I drove back to my office, I was convinced that the Watsons knew more about the hijacking than anyone else alive. I wondered whether Mike or Katy had actually been involved in it somehow, and if so, what their role could have been in it.

The coincidences were piling up – *and fast*.

Katy Watson in 1948

The Second Interview with Katy in Twisp
Robert Blevins

On my first trip up to Twisp, I wasn't sure on what questions to ask, since I had not met Katy Watson previously and I didn't know how much she knew about Christiansen. This time I had a specific list of questions and was better prepared. I double-checked everything and reserved a motel room in town.

The reporter from the Methow Valley News called my office just before I left Auburn. He asked if I had managed to see Katy for an interview. I said yes. Then he asked if I had found out anything new on the Cooper case.

Sure, I thought, *but no thanks to you, Mr Chicken.* I told him no, not really.

This time I made the drive straight through to Twisp without stopping, but the weather was so bad that I was late and they gave my room to someone else. There were no other rooms in town that I could find, so I was facing another cold night in the back of my Subaru wagon.

I went to the main watering hole in Twisp, Mick and Miki's Red Cedar Bar. I spotted a string of old video game machines along the wall. I hadn't seen Ms. Pac Man in years, and it used to be one of my favorites. For the next couple of hours I tossed in one quarter after another, swigged down soda water, and tried to forget about sleeping in the car later.

As it neared evening, I switched to coffee and took out my Forest Service map. About ten miles from town there was a road leading up into the hills that looked safe to park.

I found the signs in the dark and put little Subie into four-wheel low when the road turned from slush to snow. The road dead-ended a few miles into the mountains at a dirt parking lot for a U.S. Forest Service 'Sno-Park'. I climbed into the back of the wagon and wrapped myself in the sleeping bag once again.

At least this time I remembered to bring a pillow.

I awoke in the early morning to the Grand Central Station for snowmobilers. Several pickup trucks were parked in the lot with people unloading their rigs to run them into the high country. No one paid much attention to me.

It was still too early for a visit to Katy's house, so I decided to find some food. After I reached the main highway, I stopped at the Methow Café for breakfast. Tired and cold, I was barely coherent trying to make my order and they knew right away I was from out of town. Only the locals know how to correctly pronounce 'Methow,' which is not 'Meth-Oh' or 'Meeth-Oh', but *'MEE-Tow'*. It's a Native American word, like many of the other names for places in Washington State.

The waitress' name was Katherine, and after I finished eating I asked her if she could help me take a couple of pictures of the café. Customers were few, so she agreed. After we got the shots, I decided to tell her why I was in town. I told Katherine and the cook the purpose of my visit to Twisp and mentioned Katy Watson as the person being interviewed.

They knew Katy well. When I joked that the Methow Valley News reporter had described her as 'eccentric, but harmless,' they agreed it was a good description.

A couple of days before the trip, I had created a special item for Katy Watson, a gift that I hoped would help jog her memory on events and keep her focused on Christiansen. It was a picture frame with nine photographs installed. It held the famous F.B.I. sketch of Cooper, a picture of Christiansen and Katy standing together just before he died, a map of the Cooper hijacking flight route, and a shot of Flight 305 sitting on the ground while everyone waited for the money and the parachutes.

The display associated Katy with Christiansen, and Christiansen with D.B. Cooper. I hoped it would serve as a psychological device to open her to more direct questioning.

Besides the picture display, I had also brought a box of Milk Bone dog biscuits for Katy's little German shepherd and an old quilt for the doghouse.

Katy Watson came outside as soon as I stopped in the driveway. "Did you get my letter?" I asked.

"Well, if I didn't I wouldn't be here now," she joked. "I'm pretty busy. I might have gone into town."

I pointed to the steel giant of a pickup truck she owned. "You drive that?"

"It's the only way I have to get to town," she said.

As we went inside the house I tried to imagine this eighty-year-old woman ramming through the gears and negotiating that big truck down the road. Then I remembered that she used to drive teams of draft horses in her younger days. During the last interview, she had shown me a picture of herself driving three of these huge horses side-by-side down the street. She told me that no one had done this before, driving three abreast like that, at least not a woman. I was impressed. I also saw a picture of her running dogs in the Alaskan Ititarod.

I gave her the picture collage and she examined it carefully. "This is nice," she said. "Would you like to see what I do in my spare time?"

"Sure."

She showed me a beautiful picture frame made out of two horseshoes welded together. "It's getting harder to find old shoes," she said. "I don't like using new ones. They're not the same thing."

I had prepared a set of specific questions for this trip, in an effort to focus strictly on the time just prior, during, and after the hijacking. However, I had the same problems interviewing her as I had the first time. She continued to talk about the F.B.I. agent in Spokane, her bum of an ex-husband whom she called 'a liar and a crook,' and everything *but* the hijacking.

After thirty minutes of patient listening to this, I decided to take a chance and try to pin her down. I asked her what she was doing on Thanksgiving weekend, 1971 and how she remembered the hijacking.

"I was having Thanksgiving dinner with some friends," she said. "They didn't have a television, but I remember hearing about the hijacking on the radio."

"Where was Mike?"

"He was gone for a few days, the bum. He was supposed to go up there with me." With that, she told an incredible story.

Not long before the hijacking, she said, Mike had bought a used station wagon from a car lot near Aberdeen, Washington and an Airstream trailer at a bank sale. He told her they could use it for camping. But instead of bringing it home, Mike had driven it down to some property they owned in Oakville, about sixty miles south of Bonney Lake, and parked it.

When she asked him why he was leaving it on the empty property, he said 'I know what I'm doing,' and gave no other explanation. She said that someone might come along and either steal it or vandalize it. Mike told her to 'quit worrying.'

Two days before the hijacking of Flight 305, she said, Mike took off in his car and didn't tell Katy where he was going. Any plans for Thanksgiving were abandoned. *Mike Watson, Kenny Christiansen, and Katy Watson were supposed to have Thanksgiving dinner with some mutual friends in Sumner, Washington, a family both Kenny and the Watsons knew. Mike Watson returned a few days later and told his wife Katy he had gone camping with a friend, but refused to name the friend.

Did she get a visit from, or hear from Kenny over the Thanksgiving holidays in 1971? I asked. Could it have been Kenny who was with him on Thanksgiving?

"No," she said. "He was on vacation, but I think he decided to catch one of those free flights from the airline to see his family back in Minnesota."

I told her I already knew that Christiansen had not gone back to Minnesota in November of 1971, or for Christmas, either. His family had said so.

"Well, if you think Kenny and Mike had something to do with the hijacking," she said, "then it wasn't Kenny's fault. He just fell in with the wrong people."

I had a strong suspicion that Katy knew more than she was telling me about Christiansen and her husband, but was holding it back for her own reasons. One possibility was that she had benefited from some of the ransom money and was worried that the F.B.I. might pay her a visit. Anticipating this, I said casually that the statute of limitations was up on the hijacking and that Kenny was dead anyway. She said nothing. Katy then dragged out a big box of blue ledger books and started laying them on the dining room table. "Logs from Mike's tug," she said.

*See chapter 'Interview with Helen Jones'

She opened one of them and pointed to certain entries that listed the members of the crew and their jobs on a particular day at sea. "I was a bookkeeper," she said, "and some of the entries in these logs are phony."

"I don't understand," I said.

She pointed to her husband's name as the engineer and to another person on the crew whose name was spelled just a bit differently, but who had a different job on the tug. "Both of them are him," she said. "He was listing himself twice sometimes."

I still didn't get her point. "What does it mean?"

"He was collecting two paychecks at the same time," she said. "Not all the time. Just *sometimes*. Like once in a while. The company based the pay on log entries; the number of crew serving on the tug on any given day. I think maybe our bank was just accepting both checks as his, thinking it was a slight misspelling on the check. Or maybe he had an address he used somewhere else to receive the other checks, maybe even a different bank account. I don't know for sure. Mike never told me anything about his business if he didn't have to."

If the logs are a record of his employment with the tug company, I thought, *then the logs could also clear him of any involvement in the hijacking, since he couldn't be in two places at once.*

There was a separate logbook for each year between 1963 and 1974. "Can I see the log for 1971?" I said. I wanted to check it for his work record over the weekend of the hijacking.

"It's gone," she said. "That's one of the things he stole when he broke in here, while we were going through the divorce."

I rummaged through the box of books and verified it was the only missing logbook, and coincidentally, the only one that could prove he wasn't on the job at the time of the hijacking. *And he drove nearly 400 miles each way to get it – right after Kenny died,* I thought. *Why would he do that?* The answer was obvious to me: He didn't trust his ex-wife, and now that Kenny was dead, he wanted to rid himself of any evidence linking him to the hijacking. That was pure speculation on my part, of course. I found out later that this wasn't the first time Mike Watson had done such a thing. In 1977, he had allegedly done something similar down in Oakville, WA.

As I finished my tea and prepared to leave, Katy Watson made it clear to me again that Kenny was a nice guy, even if he *was* the hijacker. A couple of times I thought she was going to spill the whole story, and my last question to her was a very direct one: *Did she know with certainty if Christiansen was Cooper?*

She said she didn't know. I suspected Katy knew full well Christiansen was D.B. Cooper, but that if she did, she had decided long ago to take that secret to her grave. Her lifelong friendship with Kenny superseded any efforts to discover the truth. Or maybe she was frightened she would lose her home somehow if the F.B.I. began investigating her for the hijacking. It was hard to tell.

Over the summer of 2010 I made three more trips to Twisp to interview Katy. I tried several different lines of questioning to pin her down on whether Kenny was the hijacker, but I had no success. *However, she consistently pointed to her ex-husband Mike as a person who was definitely involved.* She was caught between a rock and a hard place regarding Kenny. I had presented considerable circumstantial evidence against Christiansen, but she kept trying to point me toward other people she had known as being the actual hijacker. None of them panned out. I kept coming back to Kenny as the most likely suspect, and she remained in denial.

The only person she mentioned who sounded convincing (at first) was a guy named 'Dick B' (last name withheld), a former paratrooper who had served in World War 2, Korea, and for a brief time in Vietnam before retiring. Skipp Porteous and I did research on this man and discovered he was a close friend to Mike Watson when the Watson's lived down in Oakville,

Washington for a few years. Dick B. died on the banks of the Chehalis River in 1977 after getting into a fight.

During our last interview in October of 2010, I asked Katy Watson to elaborate on the relationship between Dick B. and Mike Watson. She said that the day after Dick died on the river, she found Mike rummaging through boxes of clothes and personal papers belonging to Dick, which he had brought to their house and stored in his workshop. She said Mike got them by breaking into Dick's house after his death.

She confronted him as he was going through the boxes, she said, because although Dick lived alone, he also had a family. She wanted an answer from him on why some of the dead man's personal possessions were at *their* house instead of with Dick's family. She said he told her to mind her own business.

I wondered whether this 'Dick B' could have been a third wheel in the hijacking party, and that maybe this was another attempt by Watson to rid himself of any connections between himself and another accomplice. When Katy checked the shop the next day, all of the boxes were gone.

The following week, I asked Skipp Porteous to do a more thorough investigation on this Dick B to see if he matched the description of the hijacker. Porteous discovered that Dick B was about five feet, six inches tall, and had blond hair and blue eyes. He may have been involved in the plot to hijack Flight 305, but he certainly wasn't the hijacker. Without further evidence, I relegated this 'Dick B' to the 'maybe' category. There was just no way to say for sure.

The final interview with Katy was also different in another way. I was actually working with History Channel during their filming for the show Brad Meltzer's Decoded. The episode was about Kenny Christiansen. During a break in filming, they had asked me to take a high-definition video camera and if I could get permission, to obtain video of Katy's testimony for the show. They provided me with the camera and a release form.

I asked her a series of questions, with the last one a very

straightforward question. *Did she believe her ex-husband Mike Watson was an accomplice in the D.B. Cooper hijacking?*

Yes, she replied. This bit of film did not end up on the show, but the producers made sure to archive a copy for their files.

A week after my last interview with her, a letter arrived at my office from Katy Watson. It was a confusing message, and hard to understand. *She claimed that even if Christiansen were aboard Flight 305 on November 24, 1971, he was simply doing his job as a purser, and not hijacking the plane.* She added that I should look instead to her ex-husband Mike and some of his friends as the ones responsible for the hijacking. She reminded me of the phony log entries by her ex, and listed off several shaky real-estate transactions by Mike after the hijacking that she only discovered after they were divorced.

I had no idea what to make of the letter. There were two possibilities. Either someone had contacted her after I did and warned her that she could be in trouble, or she was trying to cover for her friend Kenny. There was also a third possibility – that she realized the truth about the whole affair was going to come out and she wanted to point the finger at her ex-husband, as he had done to her when I interviewed him.

I hoped it was the second prospect, since friendship is a more honorable motivation than fear. On an added note, the current status about 'who can still get into trouble' on the Cooper hijacking is simple. Only the hijacker himself can be prosecuted today. Just before the statute of limitations ran out in 1976, the F.B.I. was able to obtain a 'John Doe' warrant based strictly on the description of the hijacker. They continue to renew it and keep it active – just in case.

However, any accomplices are free from prosecution, no matter what their role may have been, including any laundering of the money from the ransom.

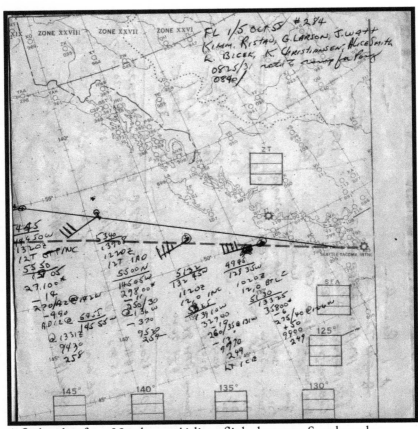

A flight plan for a Northwest Airlines flight between Seattle and a destination in Asia, perhaps Japan, or the Philippines. Kenny Christiansen is listed among the crew in the upper right corner.

Bonney Lake, Washington – Dan Rattenbury

Dan and Lynn Rattenbury are the present occupants of the house in Bonney Lake, Washington that Kenny Christiansen purchased for cash in 1972. It is now a thriving business called Priced Right Print and Sign.

I stopped by to ask permission for a few pictures, not intending to stay more than a couple of minutes. Dan Rattenbury let me snap a few photos and I mentioned a bit about our research for the book.

He said, "Aren't you going to ask me about the money?"

What money?

"The money found out back before we bought the place."

I had no idea what he meant. "You mean you bought the house from Christiansen?"

Rattenbury shook his head. "No, *after* him. There's been a few different owners since Christiansen died. One of the owners before us sold off the logs behind the house. They piled up the stumps after they were finished and the local kids used to build forts in the stumps. One of them found a bundle of twenties in a bag. I think he gave them to the owner."

"How much money?" I said.

"Two thousand dollars," Rattenbury said. "The owner took them to his bank, and the bank sent them in to the Treasury Department for replacement. He got a government check back from them later for about fifteen hundred." He explained why the amount paid out was different than the amount of the found money. "Some of the bills were so damaged the numbers couldn't be read."

The next morning I called Skipp Porteous with this information. He ran an ad in the Bonney Lake newspaper for two weeks asking for anyone who could verify this story to come forward. No one did. However, it had been at least ten years since this incident with the money and running the ad was a long shot at best. One interesting thing was the amount of the money allegedly found: $2,000 in twenties. *Two thousand dollars would have equaled one bundle of the ransom money.*

I tried to confirm this story by contacting the U.S. Treasury Department. A representative told me that they receive thousands of damaged bills each day for replacement from banks, businesses, and individuals. He said they didn't usually check the numbers on these bills, but only determined whether the numbers could be read and that the bills were not counterfeit. In that case, they would issue a check for the proper amount and then destroy the old bills.

I contacted Dan Rattenbury a second time and asked him if he wanted to go public with this story, even if we could not verify it. He said he would stand by it completely. He was certain the incident was true.*

---

* In September 2010, we were finally able to verify Rattenbury's story. A previous owner of the house, Carolyn Tyner of Colorado, confirmed it with one small difference. She said the money was turned in to the boy's parents, not to her or her husband. She says that she and her former husband Robin Powell were the first owners of the house after Christiansen's death, and that the money was found while they lived there. They did not try to make a claim on the money because they had not hidden anything out back of the house and they knew the money was not theirs. This couple had never met Rattenbury, nor do they know him now.

Notes on Working with the History Channel

Cast of the History Channel show *Brad Meltzer's Decoded* with Robert Blevins
Left to right: Scott Rolle, Buddy Levy, Robert Blevins, and Christine McKinley.

In July of 2010, Marisa Kagan from Go-Go Luckey Productions in Los Angeles contacted us about a possible show based on the Christiansen story. After some negotiations, I agreed to appear on the History Channel's new show *Brad Meltzer's Decoded*. Washington State would be the production company's final stop for the episode, with filming beforehand in Morris, Minnesota with the Christiansen family, and down in Oregon with former F.B.I. agent Ralph Himmelsbach. Once they arrived in Washington, they also planned to interview Dan Rattenbury, the current owner of Christiansen's old house in Bonney Lake.

I was a bit embarrassed about the whole thing, having never been on television before, but I agreed to do it. Two things I found out pretty quickly: These people are pros, and television is hard work. The Puget Sound segments were shot the first week of October 2010, mostly in the form of interviews between me and the cast of the show. I had some time off between shoots, and during this time I interviewed Helen Jones of Sumner twice and did one final interview with Katy Watson up in Twisp. The production staff loaned me a high-def video camera for the Katy Watson interview, and I was able to get a bit of video where Katy Watson insisted her ex-husband was involved in the hijacking. It was not used in the final version of the show, but they archived a copy of it anyway.

While the episode was in post-production I received a message from Pete Berg, (one of the producers) about some of the things they discovered about Christiansen.

The most stunning thing was that they had found a secret hiding place in Christiansen's old house in Bonney Lake, Washington.

While the crew was busy setting up for the Rattenbury interview and doing shots of Christiansen's old house, they asked Rattenbury if they could scan the house from top to bottom using infrared. He granted them permission and the crew found a 'cold spot' in the attic of the house.

Upon further exploration, they located a hiding place someone had built in the attic, just above what used to be Kenny Christiansen's old bedroom. It was a spot where someone had cleared back the insulation between the joists and inserted a sort of wooden cover, and then placed the insulation back on top to make it look natural. If you wanted to access it, you moved the insulation out of the way and lifted the cover. The film crew sent up cast member Scott Rolle to investigate and they filmed it for the show.

Of course, this hiding place could have been built by anyone who owned the house between Christiansen and the present day. It doesn't prove anything, but you have to wonder if that's where Kenny Christiansen may have hid the ransom money. The chances that Christiansen was the one who built the hiding spot are good, since he owned the house the longest amount of time; from July 1972 until his death in 1994. I considered this find just another piece in a long line of circumstantial evidence that pointed to Kenny as the skyjacker.

Another brick in the wall, as it were.

After the show aired, it was suggested to me that chemical tests be conducted to see if a large amount of cash had been stored there at one time. On January 23, 2011 I contacted Northwest Laboratories of Seattle, an organization that has been around for more than a century, and I asked them to do this. There are tests available to determine the past presence of U.S. currency, especially if a large amount of it was stored in the same place for a long time. At the time of this writing, we are still making the arrangements, but when the results are known it will certainly be news.

I write a column over at Newsvine.com, the discussion site for MSNBC. Before the Decoded program actually aired on the History Channel, messages began flooding in both to my email and to the column, asking about the show. However, AB of Seattle was under a strict confidentiality agreement regarding content filmed for the program, so I had to come up with something without violating the agreement. This agreement expired on January 6th, 2011, the date the show finally aired for the first time. I was able to post up my experiences at Newsvine without violating the agreement in a carefully-worded article:

Here's what it's like to be on a History Channel show:

They call and email you with the questions they're going to ask about the DB Cooper case, when and where you are supposed to show up, and suggestions on wardrobe. I came prepared with pictures, a weather report for the night of the hijacking, and other things.

You arrive and the film crew is unloading equipment from vans. The first shoot was at the Southcenter Mall in Seattle. The main cameraman also works for *Ice Road Truckers*. I asked him about the shot where they look up from UNDER the ice when the trucks go by.

He said, "They cut a hole in the ice and I just put on a dry suit and went down there for a minute to get the shot..." I was impressed.

Pete Berg, a producer for the show, came up and gave me a pep talk. "Ever been on TV before?" He asked.

"No," I said.

"Not a problem. We've been doing this for years and we'll help you along," he said. "You'll be fine. After a while, you'll probably have fun." (He was right)

After they get everything set up, the sound guy puts a remote mike on you, and the director briefs you on what to do. "Just stand outside the door of the store and walk in HERE when we cue you." A production assistant and I waited outside and made jokes, small talk, etc. Finally, the assistant gets the radio call through his earpiece and says, "You're on."

I walk in and the cameras roll. I sit down at this table and the main cast members of the show are already seated. I say hi, we shake hands, and then the director says 'cut'.

"Robert, I want you to do it again, but down THIS aisle instead, okay?"

No problem. I finally get it right and the cast asks questions about the case and discusses certain points about Christiansen among themselves. They shoot extra shots where you say the same lines you did previously, but they don't record the sound on those for some reason. The director orders some additional 'two and three' shots, and 'ones' which I have no idea what this means.

Afterward, everyone breaks for lunch. I joke with the cast and crew, ask questions about their work. Some of them ask me about the DB Cooper book and whether I think Cooper was REALLY Kenny Christiansen. (Yes) In the next segment we challenge a few of the FBI's pet theories about the case. Finally, it's over for the day.

An hour later, I'm making a 240-mile drive to Twisp, WA to do a last interview with a key witness. Just before I leave, they see my old Sony Handycam and decide to lend me a Canon Vixia camcorder that will shoot 16x9 hi-def suitable for television.

Meanwhile, they move on to some other segments while I'm gone. I'm not scheduled to appear again for another three days. They film at Christiansen's old hometown of Bonney Lake, and interview some of the witnesses from the book.

I get back from Twisp the next night and I have some video for the show. Since I have a couple of days off, I decide to do an interview with a lady in Sumner, WA that ends up going on for ten hours. She had known both Christiansen and the Watsons for many years, and she provided me with one frankly stunning bit of testimony that was later added to the book. When I left her house, I realized I should have interviewed her a year ago.

Associate producer Pete Berg from *Brad Meltzer's Decoded*.

On Wednesday, we do another segment in Bonney Lake. This time I am more comfortable and although the shoot goes on for eight hours and even the cast gets tired, it goes really well.

By six pm it's a wrap and they pack up to leave for someplace on the East Coast for the next show. I told them that TV was hard work, and I had a new appreciation for it. After I give my report to Adventure Books' CEO Gayla Prociv, she orders revisions to the book, to coincide with the new information regarding Christiansen and the Cooper case.

I have to say that *Decoded* seems a lot more substantial than say...*Ghost Hunters*. The cast liked to make fun of *Ghost Hunters*. When I told them they had a lot more class than GH, three or four of them held up a hand to their ear and said:

"Did you hear THAT?"

When I asked what they meant, they said it was a common line from *Ghost Hunters*, and a really dumb one.

Sumner, Washington
The Interview with Helen Jones

During a break in filming for the History Channel show, I got word from Skipp Porteous about another potential witness in the case, a lady named Helen Jones.

Our best information was that Mrs. Jones and her family had been very good friends with Kenny Christiansen and the Watsons, when all of them were living in the Sumner/Bonney Lake area in the late 60s and early 70s.

This time I was able to obtain Mrs. Jones' phone number in Sumner and give her a call. Without revealing any details, I asked her if she knew Kenny and if I could speak to her at her home. She replied yes to both questions.

Ten minutes later she called me back. "Why do you want to ask questions about Kenny Christiansen?" She said.

She had forced my hand. I usually tried to avoid telling people at first why I'm asking about him because it could taint their answers. I told her he was being investigated for the Cooper skyjacking case.

Mrs. Jones launched into me, but good. "Are you kidding me?" She said. "Kenny Christiansen? He was a good friend of ours, you know! And you think he was a criminal? You should be ashamed of yourself! There is NO way he was a criminal. And it's not polite to speak ill of the dead, you know!"

I let her have her say about Kenny and all the while I replied with comments such as, "Yes, ma'am...no, ma'am...yes, I'm sorry, ma'am." I could sympathize with her feelings about a stranger calling her up and saying one of her best friends could have been the perpetrator of the sixth-biggest unsolved crime of the 20th century. (According to the History Channel)

Finally, she eased up a little and asked what made me believe Kenny was the hijacker. I laid out a few points, and although she certainly wasn't convinced, she did agree to speak to me the following morning. I figured I was really going to get

113

the third degree from her when I showed up, and I was not disappointed.

The next morning I pulled up into the driveway of a very nice ranch-style home on the edge of town near the White River. There was a Cadillac in the garage along with a big truck. The woman who answered the door looked a lot younger than her true age, which I guessed to be about 75. Helen Jones then invited me in and we sat down at the dining room table.

I had brought a few of the poster board displays with pictures that I had used back in August at the Auburn Avenue Theatre. I had spoken for about an hour on the book and the Christiansen case. It had been a part of the annual 'Good Old Days' celebration held in Auburn, WA each year. I was only one of several writers who had spoken at the theatre that weekend. The displays were pictures of some of the evidence we had on Christiansen with explanatory text added:

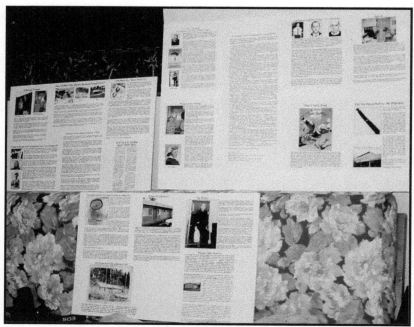

An image of some of the photo displays used at the Auburn Avenue Theatre

It turned out the poster board displays were a good idea. She did rake me over the coals a bit at first about Kenny, but she was interested in the displays. She asked if she could examine them for a while before answering any questions. I agreed, and then I decided it would be better to leave her alone with the displays while I went into town for lunch.

When I returned, she was in a more open frame of mind about Kenny's possible involvement, although she still didn't believe he could have been the skyjacker. When I laid a digital voice recorder on the dining table, she told me to turn it off, and she refused to have her picture taken.

"I'll talk to you," she said. "I'll answer your questions, but no pictures and no recordings. Okay?"

I asked her why and I was stunned by the answer.

"I don't want Mike Watson coming around here. I'm afraid of him. I live here alone, you know. If I tell you anything about him and Kenny, he might come down here and give me a hard time about it."

Afraid of Mike Watson? A guy past eighty years old whom she hadn't seen in more than thirty years? Why?

"He's a crook," she said. "That's why Katy divorced him. And I don't trust him."

We spoke for hours about Kenny and Mike Watson, but I learned little related to the hijacking. It was obvious she knew only a minimum amount about the D.B. Cooper case and even less on the possibility Kenny could have been involved. I allowed her to keep the photo displays overnight because she wanted her daughter to see them. We agreed to a second interview the following morning.

When I showed up for the second interview, Mrs. Jones' daughter, who had been about thirteen years old at the time of the hijacking, was already waiting.

I focused my questions on events around the time of the

hijacking. *Where were Kenny and Mike Watson at Thanksgiving?*

"They were all supposed to come up to our place for dinner," Jones said. "But only Katy showed up."

"Did Katy say where Mike and Kenny were?" I asked.

"She said Mike had taken the trailer and gone camping. But he didn't tell her until he got back. He just took off."

"Did Katy know if went with anyone else?" I asked.

"She never said. I heard later he was with Kenny, though."

"Are you sure?"

"Yes," she replied.

She then related some of the events that happened over Thanksgiving 1971 and a few other things that followed.

• The Watsons and Kenny Christiansen had gathered for Thanksgiving dinner at her house in 1970, the year before the hijacking. They were expected to attend in 1971, as well, but only Katy Watson showed up out of the three.

• Katy Watson was angry about her husband's disappearance, but she ate dinner anyway with the Jones family.

• No one related Mike and Kenny's disappearance with the hijacking, even as they listened about it on the radio. It did not occur to them the men could be involved. Jones said she wondered about it later, but dismissed the idea. (And although she did not do Thanksgiving at the Jones house, so did Dawn J, and she did *not* dismiss the idea.)

• Katy Watson said at dinner that she thought Kenny had made a last-minute decision to fly home to Minnesota and see his family, instead of coming to dinner at the Jones' house. (Kenny's family testified later that he didn't fly back that year.)

• I told Mrs. Jones that Katy Watson had claimed in one of her interviews that Kenny did not smoke or drink. She laughed at that and said he liked bourbon and smoked cigarettes. Camels, she thought. Her choice of brands was disappointing, because the hijacker had smoked Raleigh cigarettes. The F.B.I. found the butts in the ashtray he used and kept them as evidence.

- Mrs. Jones and her daughter discussed what Kenny looked like, and they argued a bit about it. They finally agreed that his complexion was 'olive' and he was always tanned. I asked if either of them had ever seen the official description on the hijacker. Answer: No. (The official description by the F.B.I. describes the hijacker's complexion as olive.)

- Mrs. Jones said that both the Watsons and Kenny Christiansen attended the *next* Thanksgiving in 1972. She added that Kenny had bought a house and seemed to be doing much better financially than last year.

- A few days before Christmas in 1972, following that Thanksgiving dinner, the Jones' house caught fire and was destroyed. Mike Watson moved the Airstream trailer to the Jones' property. The Jones family stayed in it until repair work was complete on the house.

- Shortly after Watson took back the trailer, he sold it to a buyer who took it to Arizona.

- Although she still didn't think Mike Watson or Kenny Christiansen had anything to do with the hijacking, she did admit she expected the F.B.I. to talk to them about it at some point. She was surprised they never did. When I told her that the F.B.I. had never investigated employees at Northwest for the hijacking, she shook her head. "I wonder why not?" She said.

- I told Mrs. Jones that execs from the History Channel show had contacted Mike Watson about his relationship with Christiansen. I said Watson had claimed he hardly knew Kenny and thought he was a dishwasher. She responded to this by going to her bedroom and coming back with a handful of pictures from Watson's wedding in 1968. Many of them showed Kenny and Mike Watson together. "My late husband was the best man," she said. I asked permission to use them in the book. Only if I returned them, she said. I took them back to my office and scanned them, taking them back to her the next day.

Left to right: 'Mike Watson' and Kenny Christiansen at Watson's wedding in 1968.

Left to right: Christiansen, 'Mike, and Katy Watson'. Photos courtesy of Helen Jones.

118

At the end of the interview, I told Mrs. Jones that the History Channel was currently filming portions of the Christiansen story up in Bonney Lake for the *Decoded* show. I asked if she knew where Kenny's old house was located there, or if she knew it had been converted to a print shop by Dan Rattenbury. *Decoded* was busy interviewing Rattenbury and going through the place with their infrared equipment. She knew exactly where it was and I asked if she would be willing to appear on the program.

She refused to go on television, citing her fears about Mike Watson. I ended the interview and went back to the Adventure Books office in Auburn to give another report to Gayla Prociv. The final segment was due to shoot the next day at the Bonney Lake Public Library and I had to appear for that one, so I prepared for it.

When I showed up for the shoot at the library, Pete Berg came up to me with a big grin and told me about the crew discovering the hidey-hole in the attic of Christiansen's old house.

That was surprise enough, but he had another. He said that Helen Jones had driven up to the Rattenbury shoot earlier that morning and tried to find me. Berg had come out and spoken to her, saying that I wasn't due for a couple of hours, but that he would pass on a message if she wanted.

"I was wrong on something about Kenny," she said. "He didn't smoke Camels. When I smoked, that was *my* brand. He smoked Raleighs. I remember because he saved the coupons..."

Berg didn't understand the significance of this until I told him about the butts the hijacker had left on board the plane.

Pete Berg also said that Mike Watson had agreed to appear on the show and would be interviewed the next day. When they first contacted him a few months earlier, Watson had denied he was friends with Christiansen and then called up his sister Dawn and tried to get her to retract everything she had said in her interview for the book. When the staff showed him photos of he and Christiansen, and other evidence to the contrary, he retracted his story and agreed to appear on the show. Berg said that I probably shouldn't hang around during the interview, but that if I wanted, they would let me listen in from another room. I said no to that, not wanting to create a scene or make Watson so angry he might walk out on the show. Later, they sent me a report on what Watson said during his interview. He had called me a liar, but he sat like a stone and refused to answer the *Decoded* cast when they asked him where he was on the weekend of the hijacking. Neither response surprised me much.

Northwest Airlines 727 N467US

Final Review of the Case against Christiansen

Can the authors of this book prove that Kenny Christiansen was the legendary skyjacker beyond any possible doubt?

No.

Nevertheless, *Into the Blast* presents a good circumstantial case to support this theory.

The F.B.I. disputes this assumption. Their official position is that Christiansen was a little too short and had the wrong eye color. But the F.B.I. has missed the target before about Cooper. Many in the Bureau once believed Cooper was a man named Richard Floyd McCoy and that assumption turned out to be incorrect. McCoy was twenty years younger than Cooper and merely an unlucky copycat. His demeanor during his own hijacking was menacing and full of threats, unlike Cooper, who according to stewardess Tina Mucklow was very polite.

Sheer luck and a few mistakes at the start of the investigation are the real reasons why Christiansen was never caught, and why he never became a suspect while he was alive.

He was lucky when he got on the plane and no one from the airline recognized him. He was lucky again when the F.B.I. wrote off airline employees as possible suspects, and instead concentrated their efforts elsewhere. He was also lucky to have friends who were able to keep their mouths shut for decades.

In 1968 Kenny attended Mike and Katy Watson's wedding. Helen Jones' late husband was the best man. After that, they didn't see each other as much until the summer of 1971, a few months before the hijacking. Katy ran into Kenny in Sumner. When Mike was gone with the tugboats, Kenny would still stop by to play cards with Katy and some of her friends.

It is possible that the planning of the hijacking was done in Bonney Lake at the Watson's house over the summer.

At that time, Kenny was living in a cheap apartment in Sumner, the Rainier View Apartments, # J-3. He had nothing in the bank, zero in savings, and no other resources other than the little bit he was able to squeeze from his Northwest Airlines job.

Within a year after the hijacking, he had shelled out $5,000 in cash to Mike's sister, and another $16,500 in cash for his own house in Bonney Lake. He also paid off the small wooded lot he had bought on a $3,000 note. After that, he purchased another empty lot behind what is now the Bonney Lake Safeway.

Not long afterward, Katy and Mike Watson began buying things as well. There were draft horses, quarter horses, an empty lot next to Christiansen's, and other items. According to her ex-husband Mike, her spending was part of the reason they got divorced, although it may have been the other way around. There is a lot of 'he said – she said' between these two, but Katy Watson struck me as a more believable witness than her ex-husband. It's also possible that both of them knew Kenny was the hijacker right from the start.

The authors of this book believe that Mike *certainly* knew, that Katy *may* have known, and that former sister-in-law 'Dawn J' suspected Kenny was the hijacker. We also believe that 'Mike' was the person who drove Christiansen to Portland to catch Flight 305 to Seattle, and met him on the ground later. That is our opinion based on the interviews and other information.

There is absolutely no doubt that Kenny's life changed dramatically after the hijacking. He never collected unemployment again and he certainly had no lack of extra money. This has been verified by his friends and neighbors alike, and it was a long-term pattern of spending beyond his visible means that went on year after year. For many of his purchases he used a Post Office box a few miles away in Sumner, instead of his home address. We believe he laundered much of the money purchasing stamps and valuable coins, although he waited a safe amount of time before doing so.

We believe that Kenny was not only lucky, but a smart investor as well. He had been poor for so long that when he finally came into the money, he used it very intelligently. Not a real surprise when you consider his Midwestern background, and a family who believed in hard work.

Two of the main arguments against Christiansen being the hijacker are his description and the fact he was bald on top. However, an article from the Bremerton Sun newspaper, dated April 29, 1972 says in part:

> 'The F.B.I. has concluded that 'D.B. Cooper,' the ransom hijacker of an airliner last November, is bald-headed, according to a reliable source inside the Seattle branch of the Bureau...'

The article goes on to say that agents questioned several people at a Bremerton, Washington wig shop and showed them pictures of a suspect. *They must have had a reason.* Today, the F.B.I. has no response to the article, even though witnesses said Kenny sometimes wore a toupee before the date of the hijacking.

As far as the description of the hijacker versus what Christiansen actually looked like, there were many variations in the description given by eyewitnesses of the hijacker. The truth is, no one has ever been able to agree that the official F.B.I. sketch is an accurate rendition of the hijacker, although it is probably close – *and it looks a lot like Christiansen.* Several different versions of the sketch have been issued over the years.

Was Kenny Christiansen really D.B. Cooper?

Probably.

If Kenny had been caught while the memories of the witnesses were fresh, would they have ID'd him as the hijacker?

Perhaps.

According to New York Magazine writer Geoff Gray, stewardess Florence Schaffner said his picture was the closest to Cooper she'd ever seen.

If he had been arrested soon after the crime and put on trial, would Kenny have trouble explaining a few things to a jury?

Absolutely.

A few months before he died of cancer in 1994, Kenny made one last trip up to Twisp to see Katy Watson. He was there to say goodbye. Katy's lifelong friendship with this man made her stand up for him during my interviews, even when she was faced with the evidence. Perhaps she was just doing what any good friend would do – protecting her best friend from being vilified after his death. One of her quotes may express her feelings best:

> *'You're not going to make Kenny look bad, are you? No matter what he may have done, he was a nice guy.'*

After his death, Kenny's family found a folder with clippings about Northwest Airlines. The first is from his days on Shemya. The newest article is dated a few months before the hijacking in 1971. Even though the taking of Flight 305 was the biggest thing to happen at NWA, he never clipped anything about it.

Account Debit		WEST ONE BANK	
We charge your account as follows:			Amount(s) Charged
Closing account due to Estate Settlen ↓↓ *of Kenneth P Christiansen*			
Date: *10-18-94*			
Branch #: *6-663* Initials: *B* Authorized:			Account Number
			1 2600 3455588
			TranCode *(Bank use):*
Kenny's final bank statement for savings. **Checking contained an additional $24,501.**		Total Amount Charged	$ *,186,276.14*

Kenny Christiansen's final bank statement. The money went to his family in Minnesota.

Additional Photographs

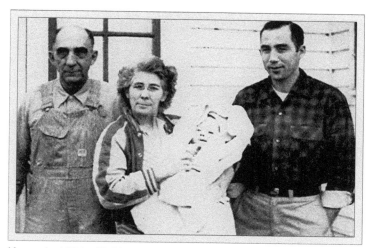

Kenny in 1954 with his mother and father in Morris, Minnesota. Also pictured: Kenny's nephew, Lynn Christiansen, as a baby. Scanned from an old photograph.

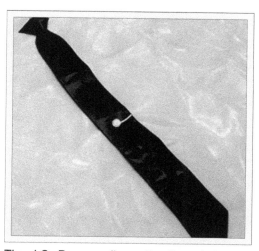

The J.C. Penney clip-on tie discarded by Cooper. Notice the tie tack is attached from the left side, indicating the person was probably left-handed. The nearest J.C. Penney store to Christiansen's apartment (at the time of the hijacking) was the one in Auburn, Washington. In 1971, you had to drive right past it if you were on your way to work at Northwest Airlines in Seattle.

Kenny Christiansen and 'Katy Watson' in 1994, shortly before Kenny's death from cancer. Soon after Kenny died, Katy's ex-husband 'Mike' allegedly drove hundreds of miles and broke into her house. He took some personal papers – *and his tugboat log from 1971, the only thing that could prove he was not at work on the day of the hijacking.* To this day she has hasps and padlocks installed on the interior doors of the house, to keep out her ex-husband Mike, whom she calls 'a crook'. She had a consistent theme throughout her five interviews with co-author Robert Blevins – she insisted her ex-husband was definitely involved in the hijacking, but denied that Kenny Christiansen was the actual hijacker. The authors believe that she was simply trying to protect a good friend, and that in reality she knows the truth. When Blevins gave her a photo collage filled with pictures of Christiansen mixed with other photos related to the hijacking, she hung it on the kitchen wall.

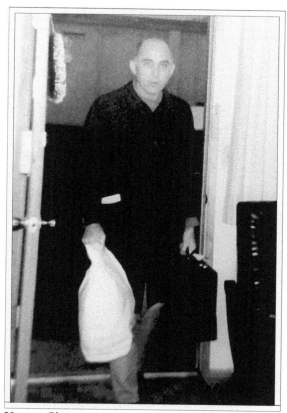

Kenny Christiansen returning to Unit # J-3 at the Rainier View Apartments in Sumner, Washington. There is a date printed on the front of the photo by the developer. Picture was taken three weeks after the hijacking, just before Christmas in 1971.

He is also carrying a briefcase and a paper bag –
the same type of items Cooper carried onto Northwest Airlines Flight 305.
The authors do not believe the paper bag and briefcase were the same ones used in the hijacking. The theory is that this is a staged picture, probably taken by alleged accomplice 'Mike Watson' and then hidden away by Christiansen as a sort of memento.

The question is: *Why would Kenny Christiansen stage a picture like this?*
It was discovered by his family after his death – hidden behind another picture in one of his old photo albums.

Katherine from the Methow Café and Robert Blevins discussing the picture display gift for 'Katy Watson'. Summer, 2010.

Fox Island, Washington State. The home of 'Dawn J'. Among other things, she admitted to receiving $5,000 from Christiansen shortly after the hijacking, and the fact that he owned a toupee. She said she suspected Kenny was the hijacker almost from the start.

Northwest Airlines stewardess Tina Mucklow in 1971. She told a
writer in 1985 that she remembered almost nothing about the
hijacking. She became a nun for several years, but later returned to
ordinary life. She lives at an undisclosed location in the eastern U.S.
today, and will not speak to the media.

Kenny Christiansen, 'Mike Watson', and other NWA personnel on
Shemya Island in the Aleutians in 1951. Watson in printed shirt.
Christiansen is in white t-shirt on Watson's right, center of picture.

4,000 MILES

Aleutian island is only a dot on the map

Shemya's monotonous tundra broken only by abandoned Army huts and airline crew

Shemya Island is only a speck in the ocean where the Bering Sea meets the North Pacific, 1,500 miles east of Anchorage, Alaska. But the island's importance is all of out proportion to its small size. Situated near the tip of the Aleutian chain, just east of Attu Island, it's the final jumping-off point for commercial and military aircraft headed for Japan using the Great Circle Route to the Orient. Shemya, which is often shrouded by gray, swirling fog and snow flurries, boast a population of 40 people, all of them employees of Northwest Airlines, which operates the remote airport. Included among the inhabitants are mechanics, maintenance men, and their families.

This excerpt from an old news article was published about Shemya Island at the same time Christiansen worked there for Northwest Airlines. After four long years on Shemya, Christiansen quit the airline for a while, but returned later and worked for them out of Seattle.

The house in Twisp, Washington where five total interviews with 'Katy Watson' took place.

Larry Carr, the F.B.I. Special Agent who was in charge of the NORJAK investigation until recently. He still keeps tabs on it.

Kenny Christiansen's home at the time of the hijacking, the Rainier View Apartments in Sumner, Washington, unit J-3.

Co-author Robert Blevins in July of 2010

A comparison picture of Kenny Christiansen and the skyjacker.

A discarded parachute, buried near D.B. Cooper's probable landing zone, was found in 2008 near Amboy, WA. After some investigation that included the opinion of Cooper parachute packer Earl Cossey, the FBI determined it was NOT the Cooper parachute, but probably from a military pilot who bailed out of an airplane in the same area in 1945. They base this on their claim that the discovered chute that was made of silk, and the one provided to Cooper was made of ripstop nylon.

There are problems with this scenario, though. No one at the F.B.I. has said for certain the found parachute isn't Cooper's, not even Earl Cossey. They use terms such as 'highly unlikely', even though they admit the parachute that was found *could* be from a Navy Backpack 6 container, the same container that Cooper jumped with from the airliner. In addition, unlike nylon, silk is a biodegradable substance and the parachute shows relatively little signs of damage or any evidence of rotting. This is more a sign of being made of nylon, which can be buried for decades without damage.

The parachute was also missing the harness and the container, only the canopy was found, and there is no indication the military pilot buried it. According to an old article in the Seattle Post-Intelligencer, the pilot built a fire to keep warm after he reached the ground, and then walked out to safety nine miles in the morning. It's doubtful he would have bothered burying it during the night, and even if he had, why would he separate the container and harness from the parachute? He did not walk out with these items, either. He left the entire package behind, yet no container or harness was ever found, even after additional digging in the area by the F.B.I.

So where did the container and harness go?

The authors offer a different theory: When Cooper reached the ground, he may have freed the chute from the harness and container, buried the chute, and then used the container to carry the money bag and the briefcase out of the area. If he changed clothes and donned the container, he would look like a guy walking along with a backpack, rather than a hijacker carrying a briefcase and a big bag of money. The paper bag that Cooper carried on the flight, the one where no one ever saw the contents, may have been a change of clothes.

143

About the Authors

Skipp Porteous is the founder and president of Sherlock Investigations in New York City.

Robert Blevins is the managing editor for Adventure Books of Seattle and the author of several books.

Lightning Source UK Ltd.
Milton Keynes UK
UKHW010629120421
381850UK00001B/165